# T. S. Eliot's *The Cocktail Party*

## By T. S. Eliot

THE COMPLETE POEMS AND PLAYS OF T. S. ELIOT

*verse*
COLLECTED POEMS, 1909–1962
FOUR QUARTETS
POEMS WRITTEN IN EARLY YOUTH
THE WASTE LAND:
A FACSIMILE AND TRANSCRIPT OF THE ORIGINAL DRAFTS
THE WASTE LAND

*selected verse*
SELECTED POEMS

*children's verse*
OLD POSSUM'S BOOK OF PRACTICAL CATS
THE ILLUSTRATED OLD POSSUM

*plays*
COLLECTED PLAYS
MURDER IN THE CATHEDRAL
THE FAMILY REUNION
THE COCKTAIL PARTY
THE CONFIDENTIAL CLERK
THE ELDER STATESMAN

*literary criticism*
SELECTED ESSAYS
THE USE OF POETRY *and* THE USE OF CRITICISM
TO CRITICIZE THE CRITIC
ON POETRY AND POETS
FOR LANCELOT ANDREWES

*social criticism*
NOTES TOWARDS THE DEFINITION OF CULTURE

*philosophy*
KNOWLEDGE AND EXPERIENCE
in the philosophy of F. H. Bradley
THE CRITERION 1922–1939

# T. S. Eliot
## *The Cocktail Party*

*faber and faber*

First published in 1950
by Faber and Faber Limited
3 Queen Square, London W.C.1
First published in this edition 1958
Reprinted 1960, 1962, 1965, 1967, 1969, 1971
Reset 1974
Reprinted 1976, 1979 and 1982
Printed in Great Britain by
Richard Clay (The Chaucer Press) Ltd,
Bungay, Suffolk
All rights reserved

ISBN 0 571 05188 x (Faber Paperbacks)
ISBN 0 571 07014 0 (hardbound edition)

I WISH to acknowledge my indebtedness to two critics. To Mr. E. Martin Browne, who was responsible for the first production of this play at the Edinburgh Festival, 1949: for his criticism of the structure, from the first version to the last; for suggestions most of which have been accepted, and which, when accepted, have all been fully justified on the stage. And to Mr. John Hayward, for continuous criticism and correction of vocabulary, idiom and manners. My debt to both of these censors could be understood only by comparison of the successive drafts of this play with the final text.

T. S. E.

*November* 1949


IN addition to some minor corrections, certain alterations in Act III, based on the experience of the play's production, were made in the fourth impression of the text.

T. S. E.

*August* 1950

# Persons

EDWARD CHAMBERLAYNE
JULIA (MRS. SHUTTLETHWAITE)
CELIA COPLESTONE
ALEXANDER MACCOLGIE GIBBS
PETER QUILPE
AN UNIDENTIFIED GUEST, *later identified as*
    SIR HENRY HARCOURT-REILLY
LAVINIA CHAMBERLAYNE
A NURSE-SECRETARY
TWO CATERER'S MEN

*The scene is laid in London*

# 1 *The Cocktail Party*

# Act One. Scene 1

*The drawing-room of the Chamberlaynes' London flat.
Early evening.* EDWARD CHAMBERLAYNE, JULIA
SHUTTLETHWAITE, CELIA COPLESTONE, PETER
QUILPE, ALEXANDER MACCOLGIE GIBBS, *and an*
UNIDENTIFIED GUEST.

ALEX

You've missed the point completely, Julia:
There *were* no tigers. *That* was the point.

JULIA

Then what were you doing, up in a tree:
You and the Maharaja?

ALEX

My dear Julia!
It's perfectly hopeless. You haven't been listening.

PETER

You'll have to tell us all over again, Alex.

ALEX

I never tell the same story twice.

JULIA

But I'm still waiting to know what happened.
I know it started as a story about tigers.

ALEX

I said there were no tigers.

CELIA

Oh do stop wrangling,
Both of you. It's your turn, Julia.
Do tell us that story you told the other day, about Lady
    Klootz and the wedding cake.

PETER

And how the butler found her in the pantry, rinsing her
    mouth out with champagne.
I like that story.

CELIA

I love that story.

ALEX

*I'm* never tired of hearing that story.

JULIA

Well, you all seem to know it.

CELIA

Do we all know it?
But we're never tired of hearing *you* tell it.
I don't believe everyone here knows it.
        [*To the* UNIDENTIFIED GUEST]

You don't know it, do you?

UNIDENTIFIED GUEST

No, I've never heard it.

16

CELIA

Here's one new listener for you, Julia;
And I don't believe that Edward knows it.

EDWARD

I may have heard it, but I don't remember it.

CELIA

And Julia's the only person to tell it.
She's such a good mimic.

JULIA

Am I a good mimic?

PETER

You *are* a good mimic. You never miss anything.

ALEX

She never misses anything unless she wants to.

CELIA

Especially the Lithuanian accent.

JULIA

Lithuanian? Lady Klootz?

PETER

I thought she was Belgian.

ALEX

Her father belonged to a Baltic family —
One of the *oldest* Baltic families
With a branch in Sweden and one in Denmark.
There were several very lovely daughters:
I wonder what's become of them now.

17

JULIA

Lady Klootz was very lovely, once upon a time.
What a life she led! I used to say to her: 'Greta!
You have too much vitality.' But she enjoyed herself.
            [*To the* UNIDENTIFIED GUEST]
Did *you* know Lady Klootz?

UNIDENTIFIED GUEST
            No, I never met her.

CELIA

Go on with the story about the wedding cake.

JULIA

Well, but it really isn't my story.
I heard it first from Delia Verinder
Who was there when it happened.

        [*To the* UNIDENTIFIED GUEST]
            Do *you* know Delia Verinder?

UNIDENTIFIED GUEST

No, I don't know her.

JULIA
            Well, one can't be too careful
Before one tells a story.

ALEX
            Delia Verinder?
Was she the one who had three brothers?

JULIA

How many brothers? Two, I think.

ALEX

No, there were three, but you wouldn't know the third one:
They kept him rather quiet.

JULIA
Oh, you mean *that* one.

ALEX

He was feeble-minded.

JULIA
Oh, not feeble-minded:
He was only harmless.

ALEX
Well then, harmless.

JULIA

He was very clever at repairing clocks;
And he had a remarkable sense of hearing —
The only man I ever met who could hear the cry of bats.

PETER

Hear the cry of bats?

JULIA
He could hear the cry of bats.

CELIA

But how do you know he could hear the cry of bats?

JULIA

Because he said so. And I believed him.

19

CELIA

But if he was so . . . harmless, how could you believe him?
He might have imagined it.

JULIA

        My darling Celia,
You needn't be so sceptical. I stayed there once
At their castle in the North. How he suffered!
They had to find an island for him
Where there were no bats.

ALEX

        And is he still there?
Julia is really a mine of information.

CELIA

There isn't much that Julia doesn't know.

PETER

Go on with the story about the wedding cake.

        [EDWARD *leaves the room*]

JULIA

No, we'll wait until Edward comes back into the room.
Now I want to relax. Are there any more cocktails?

PETER

But do go on. Edward wasn't listening anyway.

JULIA

No, he wasn't listening, but he's such a strain —
Edward without Lavinia! He's quite impossible!
Leaving it to me to keep things going.
What a host! And nothing fit to eat!
The only reason for a cocktail party

For a gluttonous old woman like me
Is a really nice tit-bit. I can drink at home.

[EDWARD *returns with a tray*]
Edward, give me another of those delicious olives.
What's that? Potato crisps? No, I can't endure them.
Well, I started to tell you about Lady Klootz.
It was at the Vincewell wedding. Oh, so many years ago!

[*To the* UNIDENTIFIED GUEST]
Did *you* know the Vincewells?

UNIDENTIFIED GUEST
                No, I don't know the Vincewells.

JULIA
Oh, they're both dead now. But I wanted to know.
If they'd been friends of yours, I couldn't tell the story.

PETER
Were they the parents of Tony Vincewell?

JULIA
Yes. Tony was the product, but not the solution.
He only made the situation more difficult.
You know Tony Vincewell? You knew him at Oxford?

PETER
No, I never knew him at Oxford:
I came across him last year in California.

JULIA
I've always wanted to go to California.
Do tell us what you were doing in California.

21

CELIA

Making a film.

PETER

Trying to make a film.

JULIA

Oh, what film was it? I wonder if I've seen it.

PETER

No, you wouldn't have seen it. As a matter of fact
It was never produced. They did a film
But they used a different scenario.

JULIA

Not the one you wrote?

PETER

Not the one I wrote:
But I had a very enjoyable time.

CELIA

Go on with the story about the wedding cake.

JULIA

Edward, do sit down for a moment.
I know you're always the perfect host,
But just try to pretend you're another guest
At Lavinia's party. There are so many questions
I want to ask you. It's a golden opportunity
Now Lavinia's away. I've always said:
'If I could only get Edward alone
And have a really *serious* conversation!'
I said so to Lavinia. She agreed with me.

She said: 'I wish you'd try.' And this is the first time
I've ever seen you without Lavinia
Except for the time she got locked in the lavatory
And couldn't get out. I know what you're thinking!
I know you think I'm a silly old woman
But I'm really very serious. Lavinia takes me seriously.
I believe that's the reason why she went away —
So that I could make you talk. Perhaps she's in the pantry
Listening to all we say!

EDWARD
No, she's not in the pantry.

CELIA
Will she be away for some time, Edward?

EDWARD
I really don't know until I hear from her.
If her aunt is very ill, she may be gone some time.

CELIA
And how will you manage while she is away?

EDWARD
I really don't know. I may go away myself.

CELIA
Go away yourself!

JULIA
Have you an aunt too?

EDWARD
No, I haven't any aunt. But I might go away.

CELIA

But, Edward . . . what was I going to say?
It's dreadful for old ladies alone in the country,
And almost impossible to get a nurse.


JULIA

Is that her Aunt Laura?


EDWARD
                No; another aunt
Whom you wouldn't know. Her mother's sister
And rather a recluse.


JULIA
                Her favourite aunt?


EDWARD

Her aunt's favourite niece. And she's rather difficult.
When she's ill, she insists on having Lavinia.


JULIA

I never heard of her being ill before.


EDWARD

No, she's always very strong. That's why when she's ill
She gets into a panic.


JULIA
                And sends for Lavinia.
I quite understand. Are there any prospects?


EDWARD

No, I think she put it all into an annuity.

24

JULIA

So it's very unselfish of Lavinia
Yet very like her. But really, Edward,
Lavinia may be away for weeks,
Or she may come back and be called away again.
I understand these tough old women —
I'm one myself. I feel as if I knew
All about that aunt in Hampshire.

EDWARD

              Hampshire?

JULIA

Didn't you say Hampshire?

EDWARD

           No, I didn't say Hampshire.

JULIA

Did you say Hampstead?

EDWARD

           No, I didn't say Hampstead.

JULIA

But she must live somewhere.

EDWARD

             She lives in Essex.

JULIA

Anywhere near Colchester? Lavinia loves oysters.

EDWARD

No. In the *depths* of Essex.

JULIA

                    Well, we won't probe into it.
You have the address, and the telephone number?
I might run down and see Lavinia
On my way to Cornwall. But let's be sensible:
Now you must let me be *your* maiden aunt —
Living on an annuity, of course.
I am going to make you dine alone with me
On Friday, and talk to me about everything.

EDWARD

Everything?

JULIA

            Oh, you know what I mean.
The next election. And the secrets of your cases.

EDWARD

Most of my secrets are quite uninteresting.

JULIA

Well, you shan't escape. You dine with me on Friday.
I've already chosen the people you're to meet.

EDWARD

But you asked me to dine with you alone.

JULIA

                            Yes, alone!
Without Lavinia! You'll like the other people —
But you're to talk to me. So that's all settled.
And now I must be going.

EDWARD

                    Must you be going?

26

PETER

But won't you tell the story about Lady Klootz?

JULIA

What Lady Klootz?

CELIA

And the wedding cake.

JULIA

Wedding cake? I wasn't at her wedding.
Edward, it's been a delightful evening:
The potato crisps were really excellent.
Now let me see. Have I got everything?
It's such a nice party, I hate to leave it.
It's such a nice party, I'd like to repeat it.
Why don't you *all* come to dinner on Friday?
No, I'm afraid my good Mrs. Batten
Would give me notice. And now I must be going.

ALEX

I'm afraid *I* ought to be going.

PETER
                    Celia —
May I walk along with you?

CELIA
                    No, I'm sorry, Peter;
I've got to take a taxi.

JULIA
              You come with me, Peter:
You can get *me* a taxi, and then I can drop you.

27

I expect you on Friday, Edward. And Celia —
I must see you very soon. Now don't all go
Just because I'm going. Good-bye, Edward.

EDWARD

Good-bye, Julia.

[*Exeunt* JULIA *and* PETER]

CELIA

Good-bye, Edward.
Shall I see you soon?

EDWARD

Perhaps. I don't know.

CELIA

Perhaps you don't know? Very well, good-bye.

EDWARD

Good-bye, Celia.

ALEX

Good-bye, Edward. I do hope
You'll have better news of Lavinia's aunt.

EDWARD

Oh . . . yes . . . thank you. Good-bye, Alex,
It was nice of you to come.

[*Exeunt* ALEX *and* CELIA]
[*To the* UNIDENTIFIED GUEST]
Don't go yet.
Don't go yet. We'll finish the cocktails.
Or would you rather have whisky?

UNIDENTIFIED GUEST
Gin.


EDWARD
Anything in it?


UNIDENTIFIED GUEST
A drop of water.


EDWARD
I want to apologise for this evening.
The fact is, I tried to put off this party:
These were only the people I couldn't put off
Because I couldn't get at them in time;
And I didn't know that *you* were coming.
I thought that Lavinia had told me the names
Of all the people she said she'd invited.
But it's only that dreadful old woman who mattered —
I shouldn't have minded anyone else,
  [*The doorbell rings.* EDWARD *goes to the door, saying:*]
But she always turns up when she's least wanted.
              [*Opens the door*]
Julia!
[*Enter* JULIA]


JULIA
  Edward! How lucky that it's raining!
It made me remember my umbrella,
And there it is! Now what are you two plotting?
How very lucky it was my umbrella,
And not Alexander's — *he's* so inquisitive!
But *I* never poke into other people's business.
Well, good-bye again. I'm off at last.

                                    [*Exit*]

EDWARD

I'm sorry. I'm afraid I don't know your name.

UNIDENTIFIED GUEST

I ought to be going.

EDWARD

Don't go yet.
I very much want to talk to somebody;
And it's easier to talk to a person you don't know.
The fact is, that Lavinia has left me.

UNIDENTIFIED GUEST

Your wife has left you?

EDWARD

Without warning, of course;
Just when she'd arranged a cocktail party.
She'd gone when I came in, this afternoon.
She left a note to say that she was leaving me;
But I don't know where she's gone.

UNIDENTIFIED GUEST

This is an occasion.
May I take another drink?

EDWARD

Whisky?

UNIDENTIFIED GUEST

Gin.

EDWARD

Anything in it?

30

UNIDENTIFIED GUEST
Nothing but water.
And I recommend you the same prescription . . .
Let me prepare it for you, if I may . . .
Strong . . . but sip it slowly . . . and drink it sitting down.
Breathe deeply, and adopt a relaxed position.
There we are. Now for a few questions.
How long married?

EDWARD
Five years.

UNIDENTIFIED GUEST
Children?

EDWARD
No.

UNIDENTIFIED GUEST
Then look at the brighter side.
You say you don't know where she's gone?

EDWARD
No, I do not.

UNIDENTIFIED GUEST
Do you know who the man is?

EDWARD
There was no other man —
None that I know of.

UNIDENTIFIED GUEST
Or another woman
Of whom she thought she had cause to be jealous?

31

EDWARD

She had nothing to complain of in my behaviour.

UNIDENTIFIED GUEST

Then no doubt it's all for the best.
With another man, she might have made a mistake
And want to come back to you. If another woman,
She might decide to be forgiving
And gain an advantage. If there's no other woman
And no other man, then the reason may be deeper
And you've ground for hope that she won't come back at all.
If another man, then you'd want to re-marry
To prove to the world that somebody wanted you;
If another woman, you might have to marry her —
You might even imagine that you wanted to marry her.

EDWARD

But I want my wife back.

UNIDENTIFIED GUEST

That's the natural reaction.
It's embarrassing, and inconvenient.
It was inconvenient, having to lie about it
Because you can't tell the truth on the telephone.
It will all take time that you can't well spare;
But I put it to you . . .

EDWARD

Don't put it to me.

UNIDENTIFIED GUEST

Then I suggest . . .

EDWARD

And please don't suggest.
I have often used these terms in examining witnesses,

So I don't like them. May I put it to *you*?
I know that I invited this conversation:
But I don't know who you are. This is not what I expected.
I only wanted to relieve my mind
By telling someone what I'd been concealing.
I don't think I want to know who you are;
But, at the same time, unless you know my wife
A good deal better than I thought, or unless you know
A good deal more about us than appears —
I think your speculations rather offensive.

UNIDENTIFIED GUEST

I know you as well as I know your wife;
And I knew that all you wanted was the luxury
Of an intimate disclosure to a stranger.
Let me, therefore, remain the stranger.
But let me tell you, that to approach the stranger
Is to invite the unexpected, release a new force,
Or let the genie out of the bottle.
It is to start a train of events
Beyond your control. So let me continue.
I will say then, you experience some relief
Of which you're not aware. It will come to you slowly:
When you wake in the morning, when you go to bed at
     night,
That you are beginning to enjoy your independence;
Finding your life becoming cosier and cosier
Without the consistent critic, the patient misunderstander
Arranging life a little better than you like it,
Preferring not quite the same friends as yourself,
Or making your friends like her better than you;
And, turning the past over and over,
You'll wonder only that you endured it for so long.
And perhaps at times you will feel a little jealous

That she saw it first, and had the courage to break it —
Thus giving herself a permanent advantage.

EDWARD

It might turn out so, yet . . .

UNIDENTIFIED GUEST
                    Are you going to say, you love her?

EDWARD

Why, I thought we took each other for granted.
I never thought I should be any happier
With another person. Why speak of love?
We were used to each other. So her going away
At a moment's notice, without explanation,
Only a note to say that she had gone
And was not coming back — well, I can't understand it.
Nobody likes to be left with a mystery:
It's so . . . unfinished.

UNIDENTIFIED GUEST
                    Yes, it's unfinished;
And nobody likes to be left with a mystery.
But there's more to it than that. There's a loss of personality;
Or rather, you've lost touch with the person
You thought you were. You no longer feel quite human.
You're suddenly reduced to the status of an object —
A living object, but no longer a person.
It's always happening, because one is an object
As well as a person. But we forget about it
As quickly as we can. When you've dressed for a party
And are going downstairs, with everything about you
Arranged to support you in the role you have chosen,
Then sometimes, when you come to the bottom step

There is one step more than your feet expected
And you come down with a jolt. Just for a moment
You have the experience of being an object
At the mercy of a malevolent staircase.
Or, take a surgical operation.
In consultation with the doctor and the surgeon,
In going to bed in the nursing home,
In talking to the matron, you are still the subject,
The centre of reality. But, stretched on the table,
You are a piece of furniture in a repair shop
For those who surround you, the masked actors;
All there is of you is your body
And the 'you' is withdrawn. May I replenish?

EDWARD

Oh, I'm sorry. What were you drinking?
Whisky?

UNIDENTIFIED GUEST

Gin.

EDWARD

Anything with it?

UNIDENTIFIED GUEST
Water.

EDWARD

To what does this lead?

UNIDENTIFIED GUEST
To finding out
What you really are. What you really feel.

What you really are among other people.
Most of the time we take ourselves for granted,
As we have to, and live on a little knowledge
About ourselves as we were. Who are you now?
You don't know any more than I do,
But rather less. You are nothing but a set
Of obsolete responses. The one thing to do
Is to do nothing. Wait.

EDWARD
Wait!
But waiting is the one thing impossible.
Besides, don't you see that it makes me ridiculous?

UNIDENTIFIED GUEST
It will do you no harm to find yourself ridiculous.
Resign yourself to be the fool you are.
That's the best advice that *I* can give you.

EDWARD
But how can I wait, not knowing what I'm waiting for?
Shall I say to my friends, 'My wife has gone away'?
And they answer 'Where?' and I say 'I don't know';
And they say, 'But when will she be back?'
And I reply 'I don't know that she *is* coming back'.
And they ask 'But what are you going to do?'
And I answer 'Nothing'. They will think me mad
Or simply contemptible.

UNIDENTIFIED GUEST
All to the good.
You will find that you survive humiliation.
And that's an experience of incalculable value.

36

#### EDWARD

Stop! I agree that much of what you've said
Is true enough. But that is not all.
Since I saw her this morning when we had breakfast
I no longer remember what my wife is like.
I am not quite sure that I could describe her
If I had to ask the police to search for her.
I'm sure I don't know what she was wearing
When I saw her last. And yet I want her back.
And I *must* get her back, to find out what has happened
During the five years that we've been married.
I must find out who she is, to find out who I am.
And what is the use of all your analysis
If I am to remain always lost in the dark?

#### UNIDENTIFIED GUEST

There is certainly no purpose in remaining in the dark
Except long enough to clear from the mind
The illusion of having ever been in the light.
The fact that you can't give a reason for wanting her
Is the best reason for believing that you want her.

#### EDWARD

I want to see her again — here.

#### UNIDENTIFIED GUEST

      You shall see her again — here.

#### EDWARD

Do you mean to say that you know where she is?

#### UNIDENTIFIED GUEST

That question is not worth the trouble of an answer.
But if I bring her back it must be on one condition:

That you promise to ask her no questions
Of where she has been.

EDWARD
             I will not ask them.
And yet — it seems to me — when we began to talk
I was not sure I wanted her; and now I want her.
Do I want her? Or is it merely your suggestion?

UNIDENTIFIED GUEST
We do not know yet. In twenty-four hours
She will come to you here. You will be here to meet her.
                    [*The doorbell rings*]

EDWARD
I must answer the door.
                    [EDWARD *goes to the door*]
                         So it's you again, Julia!
[*Enter* JULIA *and* PETER]

JULIA
Edward, I'm so glad to find you.
Do you know, I must have left my glasses here,
And I simply can't see a thing without them.
I've been dragging Peter all over town
Looking for them everywhere I've been.
Has anybody found them? You can tell if they're mine —
Some kind of a plastic sort of frame —
I'm afraid I don't remember the colour,
But I'd know them, because one lens is missing.

UNIDENTIFIED GUEST [*Sings*]
    *As I was drinkin' gin and water,*
        *And me bein' the One Eyed Riley,*

38

> *Who came in but the landlord's daughter*
> *And she took my heart entirely.*

You will keep our appointment?

###### EDWARD
I shall keep it.

###### UNIDENTIFIED GUEST [*Sings*]
*Tooryooly toory-iley,*
> *What's the matter with One Eyed Riley?*
>> [*Exit*]

###### JULIA
Edward, who *is* that dreadful man?
I've never been so insulted in my life.
It's very lucky that I left my spectacles:
*This* is what I call an adventure!
Tell me about him. You've been *drinking* together!
So this is the kind of friend you have
When Lavinia is out of the way! Who is he?

###### EDWARD
*I* don't know.

###### JULIA
*You* don't know?

###### EDWARD
I never saw him before in my life.

###### JULIA
But how did he come here?

EDWARD

*I* don't know.

JULIA

*You* don't know! And what's his name?
Did I hear him say his name was Riley?

EDWARD

I don't know his name.

JULIA

You don't know his *name*?

EDWARD

I tell you I've no idea who he is
Or how he got here.

JULIA

But what did you talk about
Or were you singing songs all the time?
There's altogether too much mystery
About this place to-day.

EDWARD

I'm very sorry.

JULIA

No, I love it. But that reminds me
About my glasses. That's the greatest mystery.
Peter! Why aren't you looking for them?
Look on the mantelpiece. Where was I sitting?
Just turn out the bottom of that sofa —
No, this chair. Look under the cushion.

EDWARD

Are you quite sure they're not in your bag?

JULIA

Why no, of course not: that's where I keep them.
Oh, here they are! Thank you, Edward;
That really was very clever of you;
I'd never have found them but for you.
The next time I lose *anything*, Edward,
I'll come straight to you, instead of to St. Anthony.
And now I must fly. I've kept the taxi waiting.
Come along, Peter.

PETER

I hope you won't mind
If I don't come with you, Julia? On the way back
I remembered something I had to say to Edward . . .

JULIA

Oh, about Lavinia?

PETER

No, not about Lavinia.
It's something I want to consult him about,
And I could do it now.

JULIA

Of course I don't mind.

PETER

Well, at least you must let me take you down in the lift.

JULIA

No, you stop and talk to Edward. I'm not helpless yet.
And besides, I like to manage the machine myself —

41

In a lift I can meditate. Good-bye then.
And thank you — both of you — very much.

[Exit]

PETER

I hope I'm not disturbing you, Edward.

EDWARD

I seem to have been disturbed already;
And I did rather want to be alone.
But what's it all about?

PETER

    I want your help.
I was going to telephone and try to see you later;
But this seemed an opportunity.

EDWARD

     And what's your trouble?

PETER

This evening I felt I could bear it no longer.
That awful party! I'm sorry, Edward;
Of course it was really a very nice party
For everyone but me. And that wasn't your fault.
I don't suppose you noticed the situation.

EDWARD

I did think I noticed one or two things;
But I don't pretend I was aware of everything.

PETER

Oh, I'm very glad that you didn't notice:
I must have behaved rather better than I thought.

42

If you didn't notice, I don't suppose the others did,
Though I'm rather afraid of Julia Shuttlethwaite.

EDWARD

Julia is certainly observant,
But I think she had some other matter on her mind.

PETER

It's about Celia. Myself and Celia.

EDWARD

Why, what could there be about yourself and Celia?
Have you anything in common, do you think?

PETER

It seemed to me we had a great deal in common.
We're both of us artists.

EDWARD
                    I never thought of that.
What arts do you practise?

PETER
                    You won't have seen my novel,
Though it had some very good reviews.
But it's more the cinema that interests both of us.

EDWARD

A common interest in the moving pictures
Frequently brings young people together.

PETER

Now you're only being sarcastic:
Celia was interested in the art of the film.

EDWARD

As a possible profession?

PETER

She might make it a profession;
Though she had her poetry.

EDWARD

Yes, I've seen her poetry —
Interesting if one is interested in Celia.
Apart, of course, from its literary merit
Which I don't pretend to judge.

PETER

Well, I can judge it,
And I think it's very good. But that's not the point.
The point is, I thought we had a great deal in common
And I think she thought so too.

EDWARD

How did you come to know her?

[*Enter* ALEX]

ALEX

Ah, there you are, Edward! Do you know why *I*'ve looked
in?

EDWARD

I'd like to know first how you *got* in, Alex.

ALEX

Why, I came and found that the door was open
And so I thought I'd slip in and see if anyone was with you.

44

PETER

Julia must have left it open.


EDWARD

Never mind;

So long as you both shut it when you go out.


ALEX

Ah, but you're coming with me, Edward.

I thought, Edward may be all alone this evening,

And I know that he hates to spend an evening alone,

So you're going to come out and have dinner with me.


EDWARD

That's very thoughtful of you, Alex, I'm sure;

But I rather *want* to be alone, this evening.


ALEX

But you've got to have some dinner. Are you going out?

Is there anyone here to get dinner for you?


EDWARD

No, I shan't want much, and I'll get it myself.


ALEX

Ah, in that case I know what I'll do.

I'm going to give you a little surprise:

You know, I'm rather a famous cook.

I'm going straight to your kitchen now

And I shall prepare you a nice little dinner

Which you can have alone. And then we'll leave you.

Meanwhile, you and Peter can go on talking

And I shan't disturb you.

EDWARD

My dear Alex,
There'll be nothing in the larder worthy of your cooking.
I couldn't think of it.

ALEX

Ah, but that's my special gift —
Concocting a toothsome meal out of nothing.
Any scraps you have will do. I learned that in the East.
With a handful of rice and a little dried fish
I can make half a dozen dishes. Don't say a word.
I shall begin at once.

[*Exit to kitchen*]

EDWARD

Well, where did you leave off?

PETER

You asked me how I came to know Celia.
I met her here, about a year ago.

EDWARD

At one of Lavinia's amateur Thursdays?

PETER

A Thursday. Why do you say amateur?

EDWARD

Lavinia's attempts at starting a salon,
Where I entertained the minor guests
And dealt with the misfits, Lavinia's mistakes.
But you were one of the minor successes
For a time at least.

46

PETER

I wouldn't say that.
But Lavinia was awfully kind to me
And I owe her a great deal. And then I met Celia.
She was different from any girl I'd ever known
And not easy to talk to, on that occasion.

EDWARD

Did you see her often?

ALEX'S VOICE

Edward, have you a double boiler?

EDWARD

I suppose there must be a double boiler:
Isn't there one in every kitchen?

ALEX'S VOICE

I can't find it.
There goes *that* surprise. I must think of another.

PETER

Not very often.
And when I did, I got no chance to talk to her.

EDWARD

You and Celia were asked for different purposes.
Your role was to be one of Lavinia's discoveries;
Celia's, to provide society and fashion.
Lavinia always had the ambition
To establish herself in two worlds at once —
But she herself had to be the link between them.
That is why, I think, her Thursdays were a failure.

PETER

You speak as if everything was finished.

EDWARD

Oh no, no, everything is left unfinished.
But you haven't told me how you came to know Celia.

PETER

I saw her again a few days later
Alone at a concert. And I was alone.
I've always gone to concerts alone —
At first, because I knew no one to go with,
And later, I found I preferred to go alone.
But a girl like Celia, it seemed very strange,
Because I had thought of her merely as a name
In a society column, to find her there alone.
Anyway, we got into conversation
And I found that she went to concerts alone
And to look at pictures. So we often met
In the same way, and sometimes went together.
And to be with Celia, that was something different
From company or solitude. And we sometimes had tea
And once or twice dined together.

EDWARD

                              And after that
Did she ever introduce you to her family
Or to any of her friends?

PETER

                    No, but once or twice she spoke of them
And about their lack of intellectual interests.

EDWARD

And what happened after that?

48

PETER
　　　　　　　　　Oh, nothing happened.
But I thought that she really cared about me.
And I was so happy when we were together —
So . . . contented, so . . . at peace : I can't express it ;
I had never imagined such quiet happiness.
I had only experienced excitement, delirium,
Desire for possession. It was not like that at all.
It was something very strange. There was such . . .
　　　tranquillity . . .

EDWARD
And what interrupted this interesting affair?
[*Enter* ALEX *in shirtsleeves and an apron*]

ALEX
Edward, I can't find any curry powder.

EDWARD
There isn't any curry powder. Lavinia hates curry.

ALEX
There goes another surprise, then. I must think.
I didn't expect to find any mangoes,
But I *did* count upon curry powder.

　　　　　　　　　　　　　　　　　　[*Exit*]

PETER
That is exactly what I want to know.
She has simply faded — into some other picture —
Like a film effect. She doesn't want to see me ;
Makes excuses, not very plausible,
And when I do see her, she seems preoccupied
With some secret excitement which I cannot share.

EDWARD

Do you think she has simply lost interest in you?

PETER

You put it just wrong. I think of it differently.
It is not her interest in *me* that I miss —
But those moments in which we seemed to share some
     perception,
Some feeling, some indefinable experience
In which we were both unaware of ourselves.
In your terms, perhaps, she's lost interest in me.

EDWARD

That is all very normal. If you could only know
How lucky you are. In a little while
This might have become an ordinary affair
Like any other. As the fever cooled
You would have found that she was another woman
And that you were another man. I congratulate you
On a timely escape.

PETER

        I should prefer to be spared
Your congratulations. I had to talk to someone.
And I have been telling you of something real —
My first experience of reality
And perhaps it is the last. And you don't understand.

EDWARD

My dear Peter, I have only been telling you
What would have happened to you with Celia
In another six months' time. There it is.
You can take it or leave it.

50

PETER
But what am I to do?

EDWARD
Nothing. Wait. Go back to California.

PETER
But I must see Celia.

EDWARD
Will it be the same Celia?
Better be content with the Celia you remember.
Remember! I say it's already a memory.

PETER
But I must see Celia at least to make her tell me
What has happened, in her terms. Until I know that
I shan't know the truth about even the memory.
Did we really share these interests? Did we really feel the
    same
When we heard certain music? Or looked at certain pictures?
There was something real. But what is the reality . . .
        [*The telephone rings*]

EDWARD
Excuse me a moment.
        [*Into telephone*]
            Hello! . . . I can't talk now . . .
Yes, there is . . . Well then, I'll ring you
As soon as I can.
        [*To* PETER]
        I'm sorry. You were saying?

PETER

I was saying, what is the reality
Of experience between two unreal people?
If I can only hold to the memory
I can bear any future. But I must find out
The truth about the past, for the sake of the memory.

EDWARD

There's no memory you can wrap in camphor
But the moths will get in. So you want to see Celia.
I don't know why I should be taking all this trouble
To protect you from the fool you are.
What do you want me to do?

PETER

   See Celia for me.
You knew her in a different way from me
And you are so much older.

EDWARD

   So much older?

PETER

Yes, I'm sure that she would listen to you
As someone disinterested.

EDWARD

   Well, I will see Celia.

PETER

Thank you, Edward. It's very good of you.
[*Enter* ALEX, *with his jacket on*]

52

ALEX

Oh, Edward! I've prepared you such a treat!
I really think that of all my triumphs
This is the greatest. To make something out of nothing!
Never, even when travelling in Albania,
Have I made such a supper out of so few materials
As I found in your refrigerator. But of course
I was lucky to find half-a-dozen eggs.

EDWARD

What! You used all those eggs! Lavinia's aunt
Has just sent them from the country.

ALEX

Ah, so the aunt
Really exists. A substantial proof.

EDWARD

No, no . . . I mean, this is another aunt.

ALEX

I understand. The real aunt. But you'll be grateful.
There are very few peasants in Montenegro
Who can have the dish that you'll be eating, nowadays.

EDWARD

But what about my breakfast?

ALEX

Don't worry about breakfast
All you should want is a cup of black coffee
And a little dry toast. I've left it simmering.
Don't leave it longer than another ten minutes.
Now I'll be going, and I'll take Peter with me.

PETER

Edward, I've taken too much of your time,
And you want to be alone. Give my love to Lavinia
When she comes back . . . but, if you don't mind,
I'd rather you didn't tell *her* what I've told you.


EDWARD

I shall not say anything about it to Lavinia.


PETER

Thank you, Edward. Good night.


EDWARD

                        Good night, Peter,
And good night, Alex. Oh, and if you don't mind,
Please *shut the door after you*, so that it latches.


ALEX

Remember, Edward, not more than ten minutes,
Twenty minutes, and my work will be ruined.
                        [*Exeunt* ALEX *and* PETER]
    [EDWARD *picks up the telephone, and dials a number*.]


EDWARD

Is Miss Celia Coplestone in? . . . How long ago? . . .
No, it doesn't matter.


## CURTAIN

# Act One. Scene 2

*The same room: a quarter of an hour later.* EDWARD *is
alone, playing Patience. The doorbell rings, and he goes
to answer it.*

CELIA'S VOICE

Are you alone?
[EDWARD *returns with* CELIA]

EDWARD

Celia! Why have you come back?
I said I would telephone as soon as I could:
And I tried to get you a short while ago.

CELIA

If there had happened to be anyone with you
I was going to say I'd come back for my umbrella. . . .
I must say you don't seem very pleased to see me.
Edward, I understand what has happened
But I could not understand your manner on the telephone.
It did not seem like you. So I felt I must see you.
Tell me it's all right, and then I'll go.

EDWARD

But how can you say you understand what has happened?
*I* don't know what has happened, or what is going to happen;
And to try to understand it, I want to be alone.

55

CELIA

I should have thought it was perfectly simple.
Lavinia has left you.

EDWARD
Yes, that *was* the situation.
I suppose it was pretty obvious to everyone.

CELIA

It was obvious that the aunt was a pure invention
On the spur of the moment, and not a very good one.
You should have been prepared with something better, for
     Julia;
But it doesn't really matter. They will know soon enough.
Doesn't that settle all our difficulties?

EDWARD

It has only brought to light the real difficulties.

CELIA

But surely, these are only temporary.
You know I accepted the situation
Because a divorce would ruin your career;
And we thought that Lavinia would never want to leave you.
Surely you don't hold to that silly convention
That the husband must always be the one to be divorced?
And if she chooses to give *you* the grounds . . .

EDWARD

I see. But it is not like that at all.
Lavinia is coming back.

CELIA
Lavinia coming back!
Do you mean to say that she's laid a trap for us?

EDWARD

No. If there is a trap, we are all in the trap,
We have set it for ourselves. But I do not know
What kind of trap it is.

CELIA

Then what has happened?
[*The telephone rings*]

EDWARD

Damn the telephone. I suppose I must answer it.
Hello . . . oh, hello! . . . No. I mean yes, Alex;
Yes, of course . . . it was marvellous.
I've never tasted anything like it . . .
Yes, that's very interesting. But I just wondered
Whether it mightn't be rather indigestible? . . .
Oh, no, Alex, don't bring me any cheese;
I've got some cheese . . . No, not Norwegian;
But I don't really want cheese . . . Slipper what? . . .
Oh, from Jugoslavia . . . prunes and alcohol?
No, really, Alex, I don't want anything.
I'm very tired. Thanks awfully, Alex.
Good night.

CELIA

What on earth was that about?

EDWARD

That was Alex.

CELIA

I know it was Alex.
But what was he talking of?

EDWARD
                    I had quite forgotten.
He made his way in, a little while ago,
And insisted on cooking me something for supper;
And he said I must eat it within ten minutes.
I suppose it's still cooking.

CELIA
                    You suppose it's still cooking!
I thought I noticed a peculiar smell:
Of course it's still cooking — or doing *something*.
I must go and investigate.
                    [*Starts to leave the room*]

EDWARD
                    For heaven's sake, don't bother!
                                        [*Exit* CELIA]
Suppose someone came and found you in the kitchen?
[EDWARD *goes over to the table and inspects his game of
        Patience. He moves a card. The doorbell rings repeat-
        edly. Re-enter* CELIA, *in an apron.*]

CELIA
You'd better answer the door, Edward.
It's the best thing to do. Don't lose your head.
You see, I really did leave my umbrella;
And I'll say I found you here starving and helpless
And had to do something. Anyway, I'm *staying*
And I'm not going to hide.
            [*Returns to kitchen. The bell rings again.*
        EDWARD *goes to front door, and is heard to say:*]

                    Julia!
What have you come back for?
[*Enter* JULIA]

JULIA
I've had an inspiration!

[*Enter* CELIA *with saucepan*]

CELIA

Edward, it's ruined!

EDWARD
What a good thing.

CELIA

But it's ruined the saucepan too.

EDWARD
*And* half a dozen eggs:
I wanted one for breakfast. A boiled egg.
It's the only thing I know how to cook.

JULIA

Celia! I see you've had the same inspiration
That I had. Edward must be fed.
He's under such a strain. We must keep his strength up.
Edward! Don't you realise how lucky you are
To have *two* Good Samaritans? I never heard of that before.

EDWARD

The man who fell among thieves was luckier than I:
He was left at an inn.

JULIA
Edward, how ungrateful.
What's in that saucepan?

CELIA
Nobody knows.

59

EDWARD

It's something that Alex came and prepared for me.
He *would* do it. Three Good Samaritans.
I forgot all about it.

JULIA

But you mustn't touch it.

EDWARD

Of course I shan't touch it.

JULIA

My dear, I should have warned you
Anything that Alex makes is absolutely deadly.
I could tell such tales of his poisoning people.
Now, my dear, you give me that apron
And we'll see what I can do. You stay and talk to Edward.

[*Exit* JULIA]

CELIA

But what has happened, Edward? What has happened?

EDWARD

Lavinia is coming back, I think.

CELIA

You think! Don't you know?

EDWARD

No, but I believe it. That man who was here —

CELIA

Yes, who was that man? I was rather afraid of him;
He has some sort of power.

60

EDWARD
                    I don't know who he is.
But I had some talk with him, when the rest of you had left,
And he said he would bring Lavinia back, tomorrow.

CELIA
But why should that man want to bring her back —
Unless he is the Devil! I could believe he was.

EDWARD
Because I asked him to.

CELIA
                    Because you asked him to!
Then he *must* be the Devil! He must have bewitched you.
How did he persuade you to want her back?
        [*A popping noise is heard from the kitchen*]

EDWARD
What the devil's that?
[*Re-enter* JULIA, *in apron, with a tray and three glasses*]

JULIA
                    I've had an inspiration!
There's nothing in the place fit to eat:
I've looked high and low. But I found some champagne —
Only a half-bottle, to be sure,
And of course it isn't chilled. But it's so refreshing;
And I thought, we are all in need of a stimulant
After this disaster. Now I'll propose a health.
Can you guess whose health I'm going to propose?

EDWARD
No, I can't. But I won't drink to Alex's.

JULIA

Oh, it isn't Alex's. Come, I give you
Lavinia's aunt! You might have guessed it.

EDWARD *and* CELIA

Lavinia's aunt.

JULIA
Now, the next question
Is, what's to be done. That's very simple.
It's too late, or too early, to go to a restaurant.
You must both come home with me.

EDWARD
No, I'm sorry, Julia.
I'm too tired to go out, and I'm not at all hungry.
I shall have a few biscuits.

JULIA
But you, Celia?
You must come and have a light supper with me —
Something very light.

CELIA
Thank you, Julia.
I think I will, if I may follow you
In about ten minutes? Before I go, there's something
I want to say to Edward.

JULIA
About Lavinia?
Well, come on quickly. And take a taxi.
You know, you're looking absolutely famished.
Good night, Edward.

[*Exit* JULIA]

CELIA

Well, how did he persuade you?

EDWARD

How did he persuade me? Did he persuade me?
I have a very clear impression
That he tried to persuade me it was all for the best
That Lavinia had gone; that I ought to be thankful.
And yet, the effect of all his argument
Was to make me see that I wanted her back.

CELIA

That's the Devil's method! So you want Lavinia back!
Lavinia! So the one thing you care about
Is to avoid a break — anything unpleasant!
No, it can't be that. I won't think it's that.
I think it is just a moment of surrender
To fatigue. And panic. You can't face the trouble.

EDWARD

No, it is not that. It is not only that.

CELIA

It cannot be simply a question of vanity:
That you think the world will laugh at you
Because your wife has left you for another man?
I shall soon put that right, Edward,
When you are free.

EDWARD

No, it is not that.
And all these reasons were suggested to me
By the man I call Riley — though his name is not Riley;
It was just a name in a song he sang . . .

63

CELIA

He sang you a song about a man named Riley!
Really, Edward, I think you are mad —
I mean, you're on the edge of a nervous breakdown.
Edward, if I go away now
Will you promise me to see a very great doctor
Whom I have heard of — and his name *is* Reilly!


EDWARD

It would need someone greater than the greatest doctor
To cure *this* illness.


CELIA

Edward, if I go now,
Will you assure me that everything is right,
That you do not mean to have Lavinia back
And that you do mean to gain your freedom,
And that everything is all right between us?
That's all that matters. Truly, Edward,
If that is right, everything else will be,
I promise you.


EDWARD

No, Celia.
It has been very wonderful, and I'm very grateful,
And I think you are a very rare person.
But it was too late. And I should have known
That it wasn't fair to you.


CELIA

It wasn't fair to *me*!
You can stand there and talk about being fair to *me*!

EDWARD

But for Lavinia leaving, this would never have arisen.
What future had you ever thought there could be?

CELIA

What had I thought that the future could be?
I abandoned the future before we began,
And after that I lived in a present
Where time was meaningless, a private world of *ours*,
Where the word 'happiness' had a different meaning
Or so it seemed.

EDWARD

I have heard of that experience.

CELIA

A dream. I was happy in it till to-day,
And then, when Julia asked about Lavinia
And it came to me that Lavinia had left you
And that you would be free — then I suddenly discovered
That the dream was not enough;   that I wanted something
        more
And I waited, and wanted to run to tell you.
Perhaps the dream was better. It seemed the real reality,
And if this is reality, it is very like a dream.
Perhaps it was I who betrayed my own dream
All the while; and to find I wanted
This world as well as that . . . well, it's humiliating.

EDWARD

There is no reason why you should feel humiliated . . .

CELIA

Oh, don't think that you can humiliate me!

Humiliation — it's something I've done to myself.
I am not sure even that you seem real enough
To humiliate me. I suppose that most women
Would feel degraded to find that a man
With whom they thought they had shared something
        wonderful
Had taken them only as a passing diversion.
Oh, I dare say that you deceived yourself;
But that's what it was, no doubt.


                    EDWARD

I *didn't* take you as a passing diversion!
If you want to speak of passing diversions
How did you take Peter?


                    CELIA
                Peter? Peter who?


                    EDWARD

Peter Quilpe, who was here this evening. *He* was in a dream
And now he is simply unhappy and bewildered.


                    CELIA

I simply don't know what you are talking about.
Edward, this is really too crude a subterfuge
To justify yourself. There was never anything
Between me and Peter.


                    EDWARD
                Wasn't there? *He* thought so.
He came back this evening to talk to me about it.


                    CELIA

But this is ridiculous! I never gave Peter

Any reason to suppose I cared for him.
I thought he had talent; I saw that he was lonely;
I thought that I could help him. I took him to concerts.
But then, as he came to make more acquaintances,
I found him less interesting, and rather conceited.
But why should we talk about Peter? All that matters
Is, that you think you want Lavinia.
And if that is the sort of person you are —
Well, you had better have her.

EDWARD

               It's not like that.
It is not that I am in love with Lavinia.
I don't think I was ever really in love with her.
If I have ever been in love — and I think that I have —
I have never been in love with anyone but you,
And perhaps I still am. But this can't go on.
It never could have been . . . a permanent thing:
You should have a man . . . nearer your own age.

CELIA

I don't think I care for advice from you, Edward:
You are not entitled to take any interest
Now, in *my* future. I only hope you're competent
To manage your own. But if you are not in love
And never have been in love with Lavinia,
What is it that you want?

EDWARD

I am not sure.

The one thing of which I am relatively certain
Is, that only since this morning
I have met myself as a middle-aged man
Beginning to know what it is to feel old.

67

That is the worst moment, when you feel that you have lost
The desire for all that was most desirable,
Before you are contented with what you can desire;
Before you know what is left to be desired;
And you go on wishing that you could desire
What desire has left behind. But you cannot understand.
How could *you* understand what it is to feel old?

CELIA

But I want to understand you.   I could understand.
And, Edward, please believe that whatever happens
I shall not loathe you. I shall only feel sorry for you.
It's only myself I am in danger of loathing.
But what will your life be? I cannot bear to think of it.
Oh, Edward! Can you be happy with Lavinia?

EDWARD

No — not happy:   or, if there is any happiness,
Only the happiness of knowing
That the misery does not feed on the ruin of loveliness,
That the tedium is not the residue of ecstasy.
I see that my life was determined long ago
And that the struggle to escape from it
Is only a make-believe, a pretence
That what is, is not, or could be changed.
The self that can say 'I want this — or want that' —
The self that wills — he is a feeble creature;
He has to come to terms in the end
With the obstinate, the tougher self; who does not speak,
Who never talks, who cannot argue;
And who in some men may be the *guardian* —
But in men like me, the dull, the implacable,
The indomitable spirit of mediocrity.
The willing self can contrive the disaster

68

Of this unwilling partnership — but can only flourish
In submission to the rule of the stronger partner.

C<small>ELIA</small>

I am not sure, Edward, that I understand you;
And yet I understand as I never did before.
I think — I believe — you are being yourself
As you never were before, with me.
Twice you have changed since I have been looking at you.
I looked at your face: and I thought that I knew
And loved every contour; and as I looked
It withered, as if I had unwrapped a mummy.
I listened to your voice, that had always thrilled me,
And it became another voice — no, not a voice:
What I heard was only the noise of an insect,
Dry, endless, meaningless, inhuman —
You might have made it by scraping your legs together —
Or however grasshoppers do it. I looked,
And listened for your heart, your blood;
And saw only a beetle the size of a man
With nothing more inside it than what comes out
When you tread on a beetle.

E<small>DWARD</small>

> Perhaps that is what I am.

Tread on me, if you like.

C<small>ELIA</small>

> No, I won't tread on you.

That is not what you are. It is only what was left
Of what I had thought you were. I see another person,
I see you as a person whom I never saw before.
The man I saw before, he was only a projection —
I see that now — of something that I wanted —

69

No, not *wanted* — something I aspired to —
Something that I desperately wanted to exist.
It must happen somewhere — but what, and where is it?
Edward, I see that I was simply making use of you.
And I ask you to forgive me.

EDWARD
You . . . ask me to forgive *you*!

CELIA
Yes, for two things. First . . .
[*The telephone rings*]

EDWARD
Damn the telephone.
I suppose I had better answer it.

CELIA
Yes, better answer it.

EDWARD
Hello! . . . Oh, Julia: what is it now?
Your spectacles again . . . where did you leave them?
Or have we . . . have I got to hunt all over?
Have you looked in your bag? . . . Well, don't snap my head
    off . . .
You're sure, in the kitchen? Beside the champagne bottle?
You're quite sure? . . . Very well, hold on if you like;
We . . . I'll look for them.

CELIA
Yes, you look for them.
I shall never go into your kitchen again.
[*Exit* EDWARD. *He returns with the spectacles and a bottle*]

EDWARD

She was right for once.


CELIA

She is always right.
But why bring an empty champagne bottle?


EDWARD

It isn't empty. It may be a little flat —
But why did she say that it was a half-bottle?
It's one of my best: and I have no half-bottles.
Well, I hoped that you would drink a final glass with me.


CELIA

What should we drink to?


EDWARD

Whom shall we drink to?


CELIA

To the Guardians.


EDWARD

To the Guardians?


CELIA

To the Guardians. It was you who spoke of guardians.
[*They drink*]
It may be that even Julia is a guardian.
Perhaps she is *my* guardian. Give me the spectacles.
Good night, Edward.

71

EDWARD

Good night . . . Celia.

[*Exit* CELIA]

Oh!

[*He snatches up the receiver*]

Hello, Julia! are you there? . . .

Well, I'm awfully sorry to have kept you waiting;

But we . . . I had to hunt for them . . . No, I found them.

. . . Yes, she's bringing them now . . . Good night.

CURTAIN

# Act One. Scene 3

*The same room: late afternoon of the next day.* EDWARD
*alone. He goes to answer the doorbell.*

EDWARD

Oh . . . good evening.
[*Enter the* UNIDENTIFIED GUEST]

UNIDENTIFIED GUEST
Good evening, Mr. Chamberlayne.

EDWARD

Well. May I offer you some gin and water?

UNIDENTIFIED GUEST

No, thank you. This is a different occasion.

EDWARD

I take it that as you have come alone
You have been unsuccessful.

UNIDENTIFIED GUEST
Not at all.
I have come to remind you — you have made a decision.

EDWARD

Are you thinking that I may have changed my mind?

UNIDENTIFIED GUEST

No. You will not be ready to change your mind
Until you recover from having made a decision.
No. I have come to tell you that you will change your mind,
But that it will not matter. It will be too late.

EDWARD

I have half a mind to change my mind now
To show you that I am free to change it.

UNIDENTIFIED GUEST

You will change your mind, but you are not free.
Your moment of freedom was yesterday.
You made a decision. You set in motion
Forces in your life and in the lives of others
Which cannot be reversed. That is one consideration.
And another is this: it is a serious matter
To bring someone back from the dead.

EDWARD

From the dead?
That figure of speech is somewhat . . . dramatic,
As it was only yesterday that my wife left me.

UNIDENTIFIED GUEST

Ah, but we die to each other daily.
What we know of other people
Is only our memory of the moments
During which we knew them. And they have changed
      since then.
To pretend that they and we are the same
Is a useful and convenient social convention
Which must sometimes be broken. We must also remember
That at every meeting we are meeting a stranger.

74

### EDWARD

So you want me to greet my wife as a stranger?
That will not be easy.

### UNIDENTIFIED GUEST

   It is very difficult.
But it is perhaps still more difficult
To keep up the pretence that you are not strangers.
The affectionate ghosts: the grandmother,
The lively bachelor uncle at the Christmas party,
The beloved nursemaid — those who enfolded
Your childhood years in comfort, mirth, security —
If they returned, would it not be embarrassing?
What would you say to them, or they to you
After the first ten minutes? You would find it difficult
To treat them as strangers, but still more difficult
To pretend that you were not strange to each other.

### EDWARD

You can hardly expect me to obliterate
The last five years.

### UNIDENTIFIED GUEST

   I ask you to forget nothing.
To try to forget is to try to conceal.

### EDWARD

There are certainly things I should like to forget.

### UNIDENTIFIED GUEST

And persons also. But you must not forget them.
You must face them all, but meet them as strangers.

### EDWARD

Then I myself must also be a stranger.

UNIDENTIFIED GUEST

And to yourself as well. But remember,
When you see your wife, you must ask no questions
And give no explanations. I have said the same to her.
Don't strangle each other with knotted memories.
Now I shall go.

EDWARD

Stop! Will you come back with her?

UNIDENTIFIED GUEST

No, I shall not come with her.

EDWARD

I don't know why,
But I think I should like you to bring her yourself.

UNIDENTIFIED GUEST

Yes, I know you would. And for definite reasons
Which I am not prepared to explain to you
I must ask you not to speak of me to her;
And she will not mention me to you.

EDWARD

I promise.

UNIDENTIFIED GUEST

And now you must await your visitors.

EDWARD

Visitors? What visitors?

UNIDENTIFIED GUEST

Whoever comes. The strangers.
As for myself, I shall take the precaution
Of leaving by the service staircase.

EDWARD

May I ask one question?

UNIDENTIFIED GUEST
You may ask it.

EDWARD

Who are you?

UNIDENTIFIED GUEST
I also am a stranger.

[*Exit. A pause.* EDWARD *moves about restlessly. The bell rings, and he goes to the front door.*]

EDWARD

Celia!

CELIA
Has Lavinia arrived?

EDWARD
Celia! Why have you come?
I expect Lavinia at any moment.
You must not be here. Why have you come here?

CELIA

Because Lavinia asked me.

EDWARD
Because Lavinia asked you!

CELIA

Well, not directly, Julia had a telegram
Asking her to come, and to bring me with her.
Julia was delayed, and sent me on ahead.

EDWARD

It seems very odd. And not like Lavinia.
I suppose there is nothing to do but wait.
Won't you sit down?

CELIA

Thank you.
[*Pause*]

EDWARD

Oh, my God, what shall we talk about?
We can't sit here in silence.

CELIA

Oh, I could.
Just looking at you. Edward, forgive my laughing.
You look like a little boy who's been sent for
To the headmaster's study; and is not quite sure
What he's been found out in. I never saw you so before.
This is really a ludicrous situation.

EDWARD

I'm afraid I can't see the humorous side of it.

CELIA

I'm not really laughing at *you*, Edward.
I couldn't have laughed at anything, yesterday;
But I've learnt a lot in twenty-four hours.
It wasn't a very pleasant experience.
Oh, I'm glad I came!
I can see you at last as a human being.
Can't you see me that way too, and laugh about it?

EDWARD

I wish I could. I wish I understood anything.

78

I'm completely in the dark.

CELIA
But it's all so simple.
Can't you see that . . .
[*The doorbell rings*]

EDWARD
There's Lavinia.
[*Goes to front door*]
Peter!
[*Enter* PETER]

PETER
Where's Lavinia?

EDWARD
Don't tell me that Lavinia
Sent you a telegram . . .

PETER
No, not to me,
But to Alex. She told him to come here
And to bring me with him. He'll be here in a minute.
Celia! Have you heard from Lavinia too?
Or am I interrupting?

CELIA
I've just explained to Edward —
I only got here this moment myself —
That she telegraphed to Julia to come and bring me with her.

EDWARD
I wonder whom else Lavinia has invited.

79

PETER

Why, I got the impression that Lavinia intended
To have yesterday's cocktail party to-day
So I don't suppose her aunt can have died.


EDWARD

What aunt?


PETER

The aunt you told us about.
But Edward — you remember our conversation yesterday?


EDWARD

Of course.


PETER

I hope you've done nothing about it.


EDWARD

No, I've done nothing.


PETER

I'm so glad.
Because I've changed my mind. I mean, I've decided
That it's all no use. I'm going to California.


CELIA

You're going to California!


PETER

Yes, I have a new job.


EDWARD

And how did that happen, overnight?

80

PETER

Why, it's a man Alex put me in touch with
And we settled everything this morning.
Alex is a wonderful person to know,
Because, you see, he knows everybody, everywhere.
So what I've really come for is to say good-bye.

CELIA

Well, Peter, I'm awfully glad, for your sake,
Though of course we . . . I shall miss you;
You know how I depended on you for concerts,
And picture exhibitions — more than you realised.
It *was* fun, wasn't it! But now you'll have a chance,
I hope, to realise your ambitions.
I shall miss you.

PETER

       It's nice of you to say so;
But you'll find someone better, to go about with.

CELIA

I don't think that I shall be going to concerts.
I am going away too.
    [LAVINIA *lets herself in with a latch-key*]

PETER
You're going abroad?

CELIA

I don't know. Perhaps.

EDWARD
You're both going away!

81

[*Enter* LAVINIA]

LAVINIA

Who's going away? Well, Celia. Well, Peter.
I didn't expect to find either of you here.

PETER *and* CELIA

But the telegram!

LAVINIA

What telegram?

CELIA

The one you sent to Julia.

PETER

And the one you sent to Alex.

LAVINIA

I don't know what you mean.
Edward, have you been sending telegrams?

EDWARD

Of course I haven't sent any telegrams.

LAVINIA

This is some of Julia's mischief.
And is *she* coming?

PETER

Yes, and Alex.

LAVINIA

Then I shall ask *them* for an explanation.
Meanwhile, I suppose we might as well sit down.
What shall we talk about?

82

EDWARD
    Peter's going to America.


PETER
Yes, and I would have rung you up tomorrow
And come in to say good-bye before I left.


LAVINIA
And Celia's going too? Was that what I heard?
I congratulate you both. To Hollywood, of course?
How exciting for you, Celia! Now you'll have a chance
At last, to realise your ambitions.
You're going together?


PETER
            We're not going together.
Celia told us she was going away,
But I don't know where.


LAVINIA
            You don't know where?
And do you know where you are going, yourself?


PETER
Yes, of course, I'm going to California.


LAVINIA
Well, Celia, why don't you go to California?
Everyone says it's a wonderful climate:
The people who go there never want to leave it.


CELIA
Lavinia, I think I understand about Peter . . .

LAVINIA

I have no doubt you do.

CELIA

And why he is going . . .

LAVINIA

I don't doubt that either.

CELIA

And I believe he is right to go.

LAVINIA

Oh, so you advised him?

PETER

She knew nothing about it.

CELIA

But now that I may be going away — somewhere —
I should like to say good-bye — as friends.

LAVINIA

Why, Celia, but haven't we always been friends?
I thought you were one of my dearest friends —
At least, in so far as a girl *can* be a friend
Of a woman so much older than herself.

CELIA

Lavinia,
Don't put me off. I may not see you again.
What I want to say is this: I should like you to remember me
As someone who wants you and Edward to be happy.

LAVINIA

You are very kind, but very mysterious.
I am sure that we shall manage somehow, thank you,
As we have in the past.

CELIA

Oh, not as in the past!
[*The doorbell rings, and* EDWARD *goes to answer it*]
Oh, I'm afraid that all this sounds rather silly!
But . . .
[EDWARD *re-enters with* JULIA]

JULIA

There you are, Lavinia! I'm sorry to be late.
But your telegram was a bit unexpected.
I dropped everything to come. And how is the dear aunt?

LAVINIA

So far as I know, she is very well, thank you.

JULIA

She must have made a marvellous recovery.
I said so to myself, when I got your telegram.

LAVINIA

But where, may I ask, was this telegram sent from?

JULIA

Why, from Essex, of course.

LAVINIA

And why from Essex?

JULIA

Because you've been in Essex.

85

LAVINIA
Because I've been in Essex!

JULIA
Lavinia! Don't say you've had a lapse of memory!
Then that accounts for the aunt — and the telegram.

LAVINIA
Well, perhaps I was in Essex. I really don't know.

JULIA
You don't know where you were? Lavinia!
Don't tell me you were abducted! Tell us
I'm thrilled . . .
[*The doorbell rings.* EDWARD *goes to answer it. Enter* ALEX.]

ALEX
Has Lavinia arrived?

EDWARD
Yes.

ALEX
Welcome back, Lavinia!
When I got your telegram . . .

LAVINIA
Where from?

ALEX
Dedham.

LAVINIA
Dedham is in Essex. So it was from Dedham.
Edward, have *you* any friends in Dedham?

86

EDWARD

No, *I* have no connections in Dedham.


JULIA

Well, it's all delightfully mysterious.


ALEX

But what is the mystery?


JULIA

                    Alex, *don't* be inquisitive.
Lavinia has had a lapse of memory,
And so, of course, she sent us telegrams:
And now I don't believe she really wants us.
I can see that she is quite worn out
After her anxiety about her aunt —
Who you'll be glad to hear, has quite recovered, Alex —
And after that long journey on the old Great Eastern,
Waiting at junctions. And I suppose she's famished.


ALEX

Ah, in that case I know what I'll do . . .


JULIA

                    No, Alex.
We must leave them alone, and let Lavinia rest.
Now we'll all go back to *my* house. Peter, call a taxi.

                                        [*Exit* PETER]

We'll have a cocktail party at *my* house to-day.


CELIA

Well, I'll go now. Good-bye, Lavinia.
Good-bye, Edward.

EDWARD
Good-bye, Celia.

CELIA
Good-bye, Lavinia.

LAVINIA
Good-bye, Celia.

[*Exit* CELIA]

JULIA
And now, Alex, you and I should be going.

EDWARD
Are you sure you haven't left anything, Julia?

JULIA
Left anything? Oh, you mean my spectacles.
No, they're here. Besides, they're no use to me.
I'm not coming back again *this* evening.

LAVINIA
Stop! I want you to explain the telegram.

JULIA
Explain the telegram? What do you think, Alex?

ALEX
No, Julia, *we* can't explain the telegram.

LAVINIA
I am sure that you could explain the telegram.
I don't know why. But it seems to me that yesterday
I started some machine,   that goes on working,

88

And I cannot stop it; no, it's not like a machine —
Or if it's a machine, someone else is running it.
But who? Somebody is always interfering   . . .
I don't feel free . . . and yet I started it . . .

JULIA

Alex, do you think we could explain *anything*?

ALEX

I think not, Julia. She must find out for herself:
That's the only way.

JULIA

How right you are!
Well, my dears, I shall see you very soon.

EDWARD

*When* shall we see you?

JULIA

Did I say you'd see me?
Good-bye. I believe . . . I haven't left anything.
[*Enter* PETER]

PETER

I've got a taxi, Julia.

JULIA

Splendid! Good-bye!
[*Exeunt* JULIA, ALEX *and* PETER]

LAVINIA

I must say, you don't seem very pleased to see me.

EDWARD

I can't say that I've had much opportunity
To seem anything. But of course I'm glad to see you.

LAVINIA

Yes, that was a silly thing to say.
Like a schoolgirl. Like Celia. I don't know why I said it.
Well, here I am.

EDWARD

I am to ask no questions.

LAVINIA

And I know I am to give no explanations.

EDWARD

And I am to give no explanations.

LAVINIA

And I am to ask no questions. And yet . . . why not?

EDWARD

I don't know why not. So what are we to talk about?

LAVINIA

There is one thing I ought to know, because of other people
And what to do about them. It's about that party.
I suppose you won't believe I forgot all about it!
I let you down badly. What did you do about it?
I only remembered after I had left.

EDWARD

I telephoned to everyone I knew was coming
But I couldn't get everyone. And so a few came.

90

LAVINIA

Who came?

EDWARD

Just those who were here this evening . . .

LAVINIA

That's odd.

EDWARD

. . . and one other. I don't know who he was,
But *you* ought to know.

LAVINIA

Yes, I think I know.
But I'm puzzled by Julia. That woman is the devil.
She knows by instinct when something's going to happen.
Trust her not to miss any awkward situation!
And what did you tell them?

EDWARD

I invented an aunt
Who was ill in the country, and had sent for you.

LAVINIA

Really, Edward! You had better have told the truth:
Nothing less that the truth could deceive Julia.
But how did the aunt come to live in Essex?

EDWARD

Julia compelled me to make her live somewhere.

LAVINIA

I see. So Julia made her live in Essex;
And made the telegrams come from Essex.

Well, I shall have to tell Julia the truth.
I shall always tell the truth now.
We have wasted such a lot of time in lying.

EDWARD

I don't quite know what you mean.

LAVINIA

       Oh, Edward!
The point is, that since I've been away
I see that I've taken you much too seriously.
And now I can see how absurd you are.

EDWARD

That is a very serious conclusion
To have arrived at in . . . how many? . . . thirty-two hours.

LAVINIA

Yes, a very important discovery,
Finding that you've spent five years of your life
With a man who has no sense of humour;
And that the effect upon me was
That I lost all sense of humour myself.
That's what came of always giving in to you.

EDWARD

I was unaware that you'd always given in to me.
It struck me very differently. As we're on the subject,
I thought that it was I who had given in to *you*.

LAVINIA

I know what you mean by giving in to *me*:
You mean, leaving all the practical decisions
That you should have made yourself. I remember —

92

Oh, I ought to have realised what was coming —
When we were planning our honeymoon,
I couldn't make you say where you wanted to go . . .

EDWARD

But I wanted *you* to make that decision.

LAVINIA

But how could I tell where I wanted to go
Unless you suggested some other place first?
And I remember that finally in desperation
I said: 'I suppose you'd as soon go to Peacehaven' —
And you said 'I don't mind'.

EDWARD
                Of course I didn't mind.
I meant it as a compliment.

LAVINIA
                You meant it as a compliment!
And you were so considerate, people said;
And you thought you were unselfish. It was only passivity;
You only wanted to be bolstered, encouraged. . . .

EDWARD

Encouraged? To what?

LAVINIA
                To think well of yourself.
You know it was I who made you work at the Bar . . .

EDWARD

You nagged me because I didn't get enough work
And said that I ought to meet more people:

But when the briefs began to come in —
And they didn't come through any of *your* friends —
You suddenly found it inconvenient
That I should be always too busy or too tired
To be of use to you socially . . .

### LAVINIA
I *never* complained.

### EDWARD
No; and it was perfectly infuriating,
The way you *didn't* complain . . .

### LAVINIA
It was you who complained
Of seeing nobody but solicitors and clients . . .

### EDWARD
And you were never very sympathetic.

### LAVINIA
Well, I tried to do something about it.
That was why I took so much trouble
To have those Thursdays, to give you the chance
Of talking to intellectual people . . .

### EDWARD
You would have given me about as much opportunity
If you had hired me as your butler:
Some of your guests may have thought I *was* the butler.

### LAVINIA
And on several occasions, when somebody was coming
Whom I particularly wanted you to meet,
You didn't arrive until just as they were leaving.

EDWARD

Well, at least, they can't have thought I was the butler.

LAVINIA

Everything I tried only made matters worse,
And the moment you were offered something that you
        wanted
You wanted something else. I shall treat you very differently
In future.

EDWARD

            Thank you for the warning. But tell me,
Since this is how you see me, why did you come back?

LAVINIA

Frankly, I don't know. I was warned of the danger,
Yet something, or somebody, compelled me to come.
And why did you want me?

EDWARD

                I don't know either.
You say you were trying to 'encourage' me:
Then why did you always make me feel insignificant?
I may not have known what life I wanted,
But it wasn't the life you chose for me.
You wanted your husband to be *successful*,
You wanted me to supply a public background
For your kind of public life. You wished to be a hostess
For whom my career would be a support.
Well, I tried to be accommodating. But, in future,
I shall behave, I assure you, very differently.

LAVINIA

Bravo! Edward. This is surprising.
Now who could have taught you to answer back like that?

#### EDWARD

I have had quite enough humiliation
Lately, to bring me to the point
At which humiliation ceases to humiliate.
You get to the point at which you cease to feel
And then you speak your mind.

#### LAVINIA

                  That will be a novelty
To find that you have a mind to speak.
Anyway, I'm prepared to take you as you are.

#### EDWARD

You mean you are prepared to take me
As I was, or as you think I am.
But what do you think I am?

#### LAVINIA

                  Oh, what you always were.
As for me, I'm rather a different person
Whom you must get to know.

#### EDWARD

                This is very interesting:
But you seem to assume that you've done all the changing —
Though I haven't yet found it a change for the better.
But doesn't it occur to you that possibly
I may have changed too?

#### LAVINIA

             Oh, Edward, when you were a little boy,
I'm sure you were always getting yourself measured
To prove how you had grown since the last holidays.
You were always intensely concerned with yourself;

And if other people grow, well, you want to grow too.
In what way have you changed?

EDWARD

     The change that comes
From seeing oneself through the eyes of other people.

LAVINIA

That must have been very shattering for you.
But never mind, you'll soon get over it
And find yourself another little part to play,
With another face, to take people in.

EDWARD

One of the most infuriating things about you
Has always been your perfect assurance
That you understood me better than I understood myself.

LAVINIA

And the most infuriating thing about you
Has always been your placid assumption
That I wasn't worth the trouble of understanding.

EDWARD

So here we are again. Back in the trap,
With only one difference, perhaps — we can fight each
  other,
Instead of each taking his corner of the cage.
Well, it's a better way of passing the evening
Than listening to the gramophone.

LAVINIA

     We have very good records;
But I always suspected that you really hated music

And that the gramophone was only your escape
From talking to me when we had to be alone.

### EDWARD

I've often wondered why you married me.

### LAVINIA

Well, you really were rather attractive, you know;
And you kept on *saying* that you were in love with me —
I believe you were trying to persuade yourself you were.
I seemed always on the verge of some wonderful experience
And then it never happened. I wonder now
How you could have thought you were in love with me.

### EDWARD

Everybody told me that I was;
And they told me how well suited we were.

### LAVINIA

It's a pity that you had no opinion of your own.
Oh, Edward, I should like to be good to you —
Or if that's impossible, at least be horrid to you —
Anything but nothing, which is all you seem to want of me.
But I'm sorry for you . . .

### EDWARD

                Don't say you are sorry for me!
I have had enough of people being sorry for me.

### LAVINIA

Yes, because they can never be so sorry for you
As you are for yourself. And that's hard to bear.
I thought that there might be some way out for you
If I went away. I thought that if I died

To you, I who had been only a ghost to you,
You might be able to find the road back
To a time when you were real — for you must have been
    real
At some time or other, before you ever knew me:
Perhaps only when you were a child.

EDWARD

I don't want you to make yourself responsible for me:
It's only another kind of contempt.
And I do not want you to explain me to myself.
You're still trying to invent a personality for me
Which will only keep me away from myself.

LAVINIA

You're complicating what is in fact very simple.
But there is one point which I see clearly:
We are not to relapse into the kind of life we led
Until yesterday morning.

EDWARD
                    There was a door
And I could not open it. I could not touch the handle.
Why could I not walk out of my prison?
What is hell? Hell is oneself,
Hell is alone, the other figures in it
Merely projections.   There is nothing to escape from
And nothing to escape to. One is always alone.

LAVINIA

Edward, what *are* you talking about?
Talking to yourself. Could you bear, for a moment,
To think about *me*?

EDWARD
It was only yesterday
That damnation took place. And now I must live with it
Day by day, hour by hour, for ever and ever.

LAVINIA
I think you're on the edge of a nervous breakdown!

EDWARD
Don't say that!

LAVINIA
I must say it.
I know . . . of a doctor who I think could help you.

EDWARD
If I go to a doctor, I shall make my own choice;
Not take one whom you choose. How do I know
That you wouldn't see him first, and tell him all about me
From *your* point of view? But I don't need a doctor.
I am simply in hell. Where there are no doctors —
At least, not in a professional capacity.

LAVINIA
One can be practical, even in hell:
And you know I am much more practical than you are.

EDWARD
I ought to know by now what you consider practical.
Practical! I remember, on our honeymoon,
You were always wrapping things up in tissue paper
And then had to unwrap everything again
To find what you wanted. And I could never teach you
How to put the cap on a tube of tooth-paste.

100

LAVINIA

Very well then, I shall not try to press you.
You're much too divided to know what you want.
But, being divided, you will tend to compromise,
And your sort of compromise will be the old one.


EDWARD

You don't understand me. Have I not made it clear
That in future you will find me a different person?


LAVINIA

Indeed. And has the difference nothing to do
With Celia going to California?


EDWARD

Celia? Going to California?


LAVINIA

Yes, with Peter.
Really, Edward, if you were human
You would burst out laughing. But you won't.


EDWARD

O God, O God, if I could return to yesterday
Before I thought that I had made a decision.
What devil left the door on the latch
For these doubts to enter? And then you came back, you
The angel of destruction — just as I felt sure.
In a moment, at your touch, there is nothing but ruin.
O God, what have I done? The python. The octopus.
Must I become after all what you would make me?

101

LAVINIA

Well, Edward, as I am unable to make you laugh,
And as I can't persuade you to see a doctor,
There's nothing else at present that I can do about it.
I ought to go and have a look in the kitchen.
I know there are some eggs. But we must go out for dinner.
Meanwhile, my luggage is in the hall downstairs:
Will you get the porter to fetch it up for me?

CURTAIN

# Act Two

SIR HENRY HARCOURT-REILLY'S *consulting room in London. Morning: several weeks later.* SIR HENRY *alone at his desk. He presses an electric button. The* NURSE-SECRETARY *enters, with Appointment Book.*

REILLY

About those three appointments this morning, Miss
    Barraway:
I should like to run over my instructions again.
You understand, of course, that it is important
To avoid any meeting?

NURSE-SECRETARY

                You made that clear, Sir Henry:
The first appointment at eleven o'clock.
He is to be shown into the small waiting-room;
And you will see him almost at once.

REILLY

I shall see him at once. And the second?

NURSE-SECRETARY

The second to be shown into the other room
Just as usual. She arrives at a quarter past;
But you may keep her waiting.

103

REILLY

Or she may keep me waiting;
But I think she will be punctual.

NURSE-SECRETARY

I telephone through
The moment she arrives. I leave her there
Until you ring three times.

REILLY

And the third patient?

NURSE-SECRETARY

The third one to be shown into the small room;
And I need not let you know that she has arrived.
Then, when you ring, I show the others out;
And only after they have left the house. . . .

REILLY

Quite right, Miss Barraway. That's all for the moment.

NURSE-SECRETARY

Mr. Gibbs is here, Sir Henry.

REILLY

Ask him to come straight in.
[*Exit* NURSE-SECRETARY]
[ALEX *enters almost immediately*]

ALEX

When is Chamberlayne's appointment?

REILLY

At eleven o'clock,
The conventional hour. We have not much time.

Tell me now, did you have any difficulty
In convincing him I was the man for his case?

ALEX

Difficulty? No! He was only impatient
At having to wait four days for the appointment.

REILLY

It was necessary to delay his appointment
To lower his resistance. But what I mean is,
Does he trust your judgement?

ALEX

    Yes, implicitly.
It's not that he regards me as very intelligent,
But he thinks I'm well informed: the sort of person
Who would know the right doctor, as well as the right shops
Besides, he was ready to consult any doctor
Recommended by anyone except his wife.

REILLY

I had already impressed upon her
That she was not to mention my name to him.

ALEX

With your usual foresight. Now, he's quite triumphant
Because he thinks he's stolen a march on her.
And when you've sent him to a sanatorium
Where she can't get at him — then, he believes,
She will be very penitent. He's enjoying his illness.

REILLY

Illness offers him a double advantage:
To escape from himself — and get the better of his wife.

ALEX

Not to escape from her?

REILLY

He doesn't want to escape from her.

ALEX

He is staying at his club.

REILLY

Yes, that is where he wrote from.
[*The house-telephone rings*]
Hello! Yes, show him up.

ALEX

You will have a busy morning!
I will go out by the service staircase
And come back when they've gone.

REILLY

Yes, when they've gone.
[*Exit* ALEX *by side door*]
[EDWARD *is shown in by* NURSE-SECRETARY]

EDWARD

Sir Henry Harcourt-Reilly —
[*Stops and stares at* REILLY]

REILLY
[*Without looking up from his papers*]
Good morning, Mr. Chamberlayne.
Please sit down. I won't keep you a moment.
— Now, Mr. Chamberlayne?

EDWARD
                    It came into my mind
Before I entered the door, that you might be the same
        person:
But I dismissed that as just another symptom.
Well, I should have known better than to come here
On the recommendation of a man who did not know you.
Yet Alex is so plausible. And his recommendations
Of shops, have always been satisfactory.
I beg your pardon. But he *is* a blunderer.
I should like to know . . . but what is the use!
I suppose I might as well go away at once.

REILLY
No. If you please, sit down, Mr. Chamberlayne.
You are not going away, so you might as well sit down.
You were going to ask a question.

EDWARD
                            When you came to my flat
Had you been invited by my wife as a guest
As I supposed? . . . Or did she *send* you?

REILLY
I cannot say that I had been invited;
And Mrs. Chamberlayne did not know that I was coming.
But I knew you would be there, and whom I should find
        with you.

EDWARD
But you had seen my wife?

REILLY
                    Oh yes, I had seen her.

107

EDWARD

So this *is* a trap!

REILLY

Let's not call it a trap.
But if it is a trap, then you cannot escape from it:
And so . . . you might as well sit down.
I think you will find that chair comfortable.

EDWARD

You knew,
Before I began to tell you, what had happened?

REILLY

That is so, that is so. But all in good time.
Let us dismiss that question for the moment.
Tell me first, about the difficulties
On which you want my professional opinion.

EDWARD

It's not for me to blame you for bringing my wife back,
I suppose. You seemed to be trying to persuade me
That I was better off without her. But didn't you realise
That I was in no state to make a decision?

REILLY

If I had not brought your wife back, Mr. Chamberlayne,
Do you suppose that things would be any better — now?

EDWARD

I don't know, I'm sure. They could hardly be worse.

REILLY

They might be much worse. You might have ruined three
lives

By your indecision. Now there are only two —
Which you still have the chance of redeeming from ruin.

#### EDWARD

You talk as if I was capable of action:
If I were, I should not need to consult you
Or anyone else. I came here as a patient.
If you take no interest in my case, I can go elsewhere.

#### REILLY

You have reason to believe that you are very ill?

#### EDWARD

I should have thought a doctor could see that for himself.
Or at least that he would enquire about the symptoms.
Two people advised me recently,
Almost in the same words, that I ought to see a doctor.
They said — again, in almost the same words —
That I was on the edge of a nervous breakdown.
I didn't know it then myself — but if they saw it
I should have thought that a doctor could see it.

#### REILLY

'Nervous breakdown' is a term I never use:
It can mean almost anything.

#### EDWARD

                    And since then, I have realised
That mine is a very unusual case.

#### REILLY

All cases are unique, and very similar to others.

#### EDWARD

Is there a sanatorium to which you send such patients

109

As myself, under your personal observation?


REILLY

You are very impetuous, Mr. Chamberlayne.
There are several kinds of sanatoria
For several kinds of patient. And there are also patients
For whom a sanatorium is the worst place possible.
We must first find out what is wrong with you
Before we decide what to do with you.


EDWARD

I doubt if you have ever had a case like mine:
I have ceased to believe in my own personality.


REILLY

Oh, dear yes; this is serious. A very common malady.
Very prevalent indeed.


EDWARD

I remember, in my childhood . . .


REILLY

I always begin from the immediate situation
And then go back as far as I find necessary.
You see, your memories of childhood —
I mean, in your present state of mind —
Would be largely fictitious; and as for your dreams,
You would produce amazing dreams, to oblige me.
I could make you dream any kind of dream I suggested,
And it would only go to flatter your vanity
With the temporary stimulus of feeling interesting.

110

EDWARD

But I am obsessed by the thought of my own insignificance.

REILLY

Precisely. And I could make you feel important,
And you would imagine it a marvellous cure;
And you would go on, doing such amount of mischief
As lay within your power — until you came to grief.
Half of the harm that is done in this world
Is due to people who want to feel important.
They don't mean to do harm — but the harm does not
    interest them.
Or they do not see it, or they justify it
Because they are absorbed in the endless struggle
To think well of themselves.

EDWARD

                    If I am like that
I must have done a great deal of harm.

REILLY

Oh, not so much as you would like to think:
Only, shall we say, within your modest capacity.
Try to explain what has happened since I left you.

EDWARD

I see now why I wanted my wife to come back.
It was because of what she had made me into.
We had not been alone again for fifteen minutes
Before I felt, and still more acutely —
Indeed, acutely, perhaps, for the first time,
The whole oppression, the unreality
Of the role she had always imposed upon me
With the obstinate, unconscious, sub-human strength

That some women have. Without her, it was vacancy.
When I thought she had left me, I began to dissolve,
To cease to exist. That was what she had done to me!
I cannot live with her — that is now intolerable;
I cannot live without her, for she has made me incapable
Of having any existence of my own.
That is what she has done to me in five years together!
She has made the world a place I cannot live in
Except on her terms. I must be alone,
But not in the same world. So I want you to put me
Into your sanatorium. I could be alone there?
                    [*House-telephone rings*]


                        REILLY
[*Into telephone*]    Yes.
[*To* EDWARD]                        Yes, you could be alone there.


                        EDWARD
                                    I wonder
If you have understood a word of what I have been saying.


                        REILLY
You must have patience with me, Mr. Chamberlayne:
I learn a good deal by merely observing you,
And letting you talk as long as you please,
And taking note of what you do not say.


                        EDWARD
I once experienced the extreme of physical pain,
And now I know there is suffering worse than that.
It is surprising, if one had time to be surprised:
I am not afraid of the death of the body,
But this death is terrifying. The death of the spirit —
Can you understand what I suffer?

112

REILLY
                    I understand what you mean.

EDWARD
I can no longer act for myself.
Coming to see you — that's the last decision
I was capable of making. I am in your hands.
I cannot take any further responsibility.

REILLY
Many patients come in that belief.

EDWARD
And now will you send me to the sanatorium?

REILLY
You have nothing else to tell me?

EDWARD
                    What else can I tell you?
You didn't want to hear about my early history.

REILLY
No, I did not want to hear about your *early* history.

EDWARD
And so will you send me to the sanatorium?
I can't go home again. And at my club
They won't let you keep a room for more than seven days;
I haven't the courage to go to a hotel,
And besides, I need more shirts — you can get my wife
To have my things sent on: whatever I shall need.
But of course you mustn't tell her where I am.
Is it far to go?

REILLY

You might say, a long journey.
But before I treat a patient like yourself
I need to know a great deal more about him,
Than the patient himself can always tell me.
Indeed, it is often the case that my patients
Are only pieces of a total situation
Which I have to explore. The single patient
Who is ill by himself, is rather the exception.
I have recently had another patient
Whose situation is much the same as your own.

[*Presses the bell on his desk three times*]

You must accept a rather unusual procedure:
I propose to introduce you to the other patient.

EDWARD

What do you mean? Who is this other patient?
I consider this very unprofessional conduct —
I will not discuss my case before another patient.

REILLY

On the contrary. That is the only way
In which it can be discussed. You have told me nothing.
You have had the opportunity, and you have said enough
To convince me that you have been making up your case
So to speak, as you went along. A barrister
Ought to know his brief before he enters the court.

EDWARD

I am at least free to leave. And I propose to do so.
My mind is made up. I shall go to a hotel.

REILLY

It is just because you are not free, Mr. Chamberlayne,

That you have come to me. It is for me to give you that —
Your freedom. That is my affair.
          [LAVINIA *is shown in by the* NURSE-SECRETARY]
But here is the other patient.

EDWARD
Lavinia!

LAVINIA
                                   Well, Sir Henry!
I said I would come to talk about my husband:
I didn't say I was prepared to meet him.

EDWARD
And I did not expect to meet *you*, Lavinia.
I call this a very dishonourable trick.

REILLY
Honesty before honour,   Mr. Chamberlayne.
Sit down, please, both of you. Mrs. Chamberlayne,
Your husband wishes to enter a sanatorium,
And that is a question which naturally concerns you.

EDWARD
I am not going to any sanatorium.
I am going to a hotel. And I shall ask you, Lavinia,
To be so good as to send me on some clothes.

LAVINIA
Oh, to what hotel?

EDWARD
          I don't know — I mean to say,
That doesn't concern you.

115

LAVINIA
                    In that case, Edward,
I don't think your clothes concern me either.
                    [*To* REILLY]
I presume you will send him to the same sanatorium
To which you sent me? Well, he needs it more than I did.

REILLY
I am glad that you have come to see it in that light —
At least, for the moment. But, Mrs. Chamberlayne,
You have never visited my sanatorium.

LAVINIA
What do you mean? I asked to be sent
And you took me there. If that was not a sanatorium
What was it?

REILLY
                    A kind of hotel. A retreat
For people who imagine that they need a respite
From everyday life. They return refreshed;
And if they believe it to be a sanatorium
That is good reason for not sending them to one.
The people who need my sort of sanatorium
Are not easily deceived.

LAVINIA
                    Are you a devil
Or merely a lunatic practical joker?

EDWARD
I incline to the second explanation
Without the qualification 'lunatic'.
Why should *you* go to a sanatorium?

116

I have never known anyone in my life
With fewer mental complications than you;
You're stronger than a . . . battleship. That's what drove me
    mad.
I am the one who needs a sanatorium —
But I'm not going there.

#### REILLY
        You are right, Mr. Chamberlayne.
You are no case for my sanatorium:
You are much too ill.

#### EDWARD
        Much too ill?
Then I'll go and be ill in a suburban boarding-house.

#### LAVINIA
That would never suit you, Edward. Now I know of a hotel
In the New Forest . . .

#### EDWARD
        How like you, Lavinia.
You always know of something better.

#### LAVINIA
It's only that I have a more practical mind
Than you have, Edward. You do know that.

#### EDWARD
Only because you've told me so often.
I'd like to see *you* filling up an income-tax form.

#### LAVINIA
Don't be silly, Edward. When I say practical,
I mean practical in the things that really matter.

REILLY

May I interrupt this interesting discussion?
I say you are both too ill. There several symptoms
Which must occur together, and to a marked degree,
To qualify a patient for *my* sanatorium:
And one of them is an honest mind.
That is one of the causes of their suffering.

LAVINIA

No one can say my husband has an honest mind.

EDWARD

And I could not honestly say that of *you*, Lavinia.

REILLY

I congratulate you both on your perspicacity.
Your sympathetic understanding of each other
Will prepare you to appreciate what I have to say to you.
I do not trouble myself with the common cheat,
Or with the insuperably, innocently dull:
My patients such as you are the self-deceivers
Taking infinite pains, exhausting their energy,
Yet never quite successful. You have both of you pretended
To be consulting me; both, tried to impose upon me
Your own diagnosis, and prescribe your own cure.
But when you put yourselves into hands like mine
You surrender a great deal more than you meant to.
This is the consequence of trying to lie to me.

LAVINIA

I did not come here to be insulted.

REILLY

You have come where the word 'insult' has no meaning;

And you must put up with that. All that you have told me —
Both of you — was true enough: you described your
　　　feelings —
Or some of them — omitting the important facts.
Let me take your husband first.
　　　　　　　[*To* EDWARD]
　　　　　　　　　　　　You were lying to me
By concealing your relations with Miss Coplestone.

EDWARD

This is monstrous! My wife knew nothing about it.

LAVINIA

Really, Edward! Even if I'd been blind
There were plenty of people to let me know about it.
I wonder if there was anyone who didn't know.

REILLY

There was one, in fact.　But you, Mrs. Chamberlayne,
Tried to make me believe that it was this discovery
Precipitated what you called your nervous breakdown.

LAVINIA

But it's true! I was completely prostrated;
Even if I have made a partial recovery.

REILLY

Certainly, you were completely prostrated,
And certainly, you have somewhat recovered.
But you failed to mention that the cause of your distress
Was the defection of your lover — who suddenly
For the first time in his life, fell in love with someone,
And with someone of whom you had reason to be jealous.

EDWARD

Really, Lavinia! This is very interesting.
You seem to have been much more successful at concealment
Than I was. Now I wonder who it could have been.

LAVINIA

Well, tell him if you like.

REILLY

A young man named Peter.

EDWARD

Peter? Peter who?

REILLY

Mr. Peter Quilpe
Was a frequent guest.

EDWARD

Peter Quilpe.
Peter Quilpe! Really Lavinia!
I congratulate you. You could not have chosen
Anyone I was less likely to suspect.
And then he came to *me* to confide about Celia!
I have never heard anything so utterly ludicrous:
This is the best joke that ever happened.

LAVINIA

I never knew you had such a sense of humour.

REILLY

It is the first more hopeful symptom.

LAVINIA

How did you know all this?

REILLY
                    That I cannot disclose.
I have my own method of collecting information
About my patients. You must not ask me to reveal it —
That is a matter of professional etiquette.

LAVINIA
I have not noticed much professional etiquette
About your behaviour to-day.

REILLY
                    A point well taken.
But permit me to remark that my revelations
About each of you, to one another,
Have not been of anything that you confided to me.
The information I have exchanged between you
Was all obtained from outside sources.
Mrs. Chamberlayne, when you came to me two months ago
I was dissatisfied with your explanation
Of your obvious symptoms of emotional strain
And so I made enquiries.

EDWARD
                    It was two months ago
That your breakdown began! And I never noticed it.

LAVINIA
You wouldn't notice anything. You never noticed *me*.

REILLY
Now, I want to point out to both of you
How much you have in common. Indeed, I consider
That you are exceptionally well-suited to each other.

121

Mr. Chamberlayne, when you thought your wife had left
    you,
You discovered, to your surprise and consternation,
That you were not really in love with Miss Coplestone . . .

LAVINIA

My husband has never been in love with anybody.

REILLY

And were not prepared to make the least sacrifice
On her account. This injured your vanity.
You liked to think of yourself as a passionate lover.
Then you realised, what your wife has justly remarked,
That you had never been in love with anybody;
Which made you suspect that you were incapable
Of loving. To men of a certain type
The suspicion that they are incapable of loving
Is as disturbing to their self-esteem
As, in cruder men, the fear of impotence.

LAVINIA

You *are* cold-hearted, Edward.

REILLY

                So you say, Mrs. Chamberlayne.
And now, let us turn to your side of the problem.
When you discovered that your young friend
(Though you knew, in your heart, that he was not in love
    with you,
And were always humiliated by the awareness
That you had forced him into this position) —
When, I say, you discovered that your young friend
Had actually fallen in love with Miss Coplestone,
It took you some time, I have no doubt,

Before you would admit it. Though perhaps you knew it
Before he did. You pretended to yourself,
I suspect, and for as long as you could,
That he was aiming at a higher social distinction
Than the honour conferred by being *your* lover.
When you had to face the fact that his feelings towards her
Were different from any you had aroused in him —
It was a shock. You had wanted to be loved;
You had come to see that no one had ever loved you.
Then you began to fear that no one *could* love you.

EDWARD

I'm beginning to feel very sorry for you, Lavinia.
You know, you really are exceptionally unlovable,
And I never quite knew why. I thought it was *my* fault.

REILLY

And now you begin to see, I hope,
How much you have in common. The same isolation.
A man who finds himself incapable of loving
And a woman who finds that no man can love her.

LAVINIA

It seems to me that what we have in common
Might be just enough to make us loathe one another.

REILLY

See it rather as the bond which holds you together.
While still in a state of unenlightenment,
*You* could always say: 'he could not love any woman;'
*You* could always say: 'no man could love her.'
You could accuse each other of your own faults,
And so could avoid understanding each other.
Now, you have only to reverse the propositions
And put them together.

LAVINIA
Is that possible?

REILLY
If I had sent either of you to the sanatorium
In the state in which you came to me — I tell you this:
It would have been a horror beyond your imagining,
For you would have been left with what you brought with
    you:
The shadow of desires of desires.   A prey
To the devils who arrive at their plenitude of power
When they have you to themselves.

LAVINIA
                Then what can we do
When we can go neither back nor forward? Edward!
What can we do?

REILLY
           You have answered your own question,
Though you do not know the meaning of what you have
   said.

EDWARD
Lavinia, we must make the best of a bad job.
That is what he means.

REILLY
           When you find, Mr. Chamberlayne,
The best of a bad job is all any of us make of it —
Except of course, the saints — such as those who go
To the sanatorium — you will forget this phrase,
And in forgetting it will alter the condition.

LAVINIA

Edward, there *is* that hotel in the New Forest
If you want to go there. The proprietor
Who has just taken over, is a friend of Alex's.
I could go down with you, and then leave you there
If you want to be alone . . .

EDWARD

But I can't go away!
I have a case coming on next Monday.

LAVINIA

Then will you stop at your club?

EDWARD

No, they won't let me.
I must leave tomorrow — but how did you know
I was staying at the club?

LAVINIA

Really, Edward!
I have *some* sense of responsibility.
I was going to leave some shirts there for you.

EDWARD

It seems to me that I might as well go home.

LAVINIA

Then we can share a taxi, and be economical.
Edward, have you anything else to ask him
Before we go?

EDWARD

Yes, I have.
But it's difficult to say.

125

LAVINIA

But I wish you would say it.
At least, there is something I would like you to ask.

EDWARD

It's about the future of . . . the others.
I don't want to build on other people's ruins.

LAVINIA

Exactly. And I have a question too.
Sir Henry, was it you who sent those telegrams?

REILLY

I think I will dispose of your husband's problem.
[*To* EDWARD]
Your business is not to clear your conscience
But to learn how to bear the burdens on your conscience.
With the future of the others you are not concerned.

LAVINIA

I think you have answered my question too.
They had to tell us, themselves, that they had made their
    decision.

EDWARD

Have you anything else to say to us, Sir Henry?

REILLY

No. Not in this capacity.
[EDWARD *takes out his cheque-book.* REILLY *raises his hand.*]
My secretary will send you my account.
Go in peace. And work out your salvation with diligence.
                    [*Exeunt* EDWARD *and* LAVINIA]
[REILLY *goes to the couch and lies down. The house-telephone
    rings. He gets up and answers it.*]

126

REILLY

Yes? . . . Yes. Come in.
[*Enter* JULIA *by side door*]
                    She's waiting downstairs.

JULIA

I know that, Henry. I brought her here myself.

REILLY

Oh? You didn't let her know you were seeing me first?

JULIA

Of course not. I dropped her at the door
And went on in the taxi, round the corner;
Waited a moment, and slipped in by the back way.
I only came to tell you, I am sure she is ready
To make a decision.

REILLY

                    Was she reluctant?
Was that why you brought her?

JULIA

                                        Oh no, not reluctant:
Only diffident. She cannot believe
That you will take her seriously.

REILLY

                                        That is not uncommon.

JULIA

Or that she deserves to be taken seriously.

REILLY

That is most uncommon.

127

JULIA

Henry, get up.
You can't be as tired as that. I shall wait in the next room,
And come back when she's gone.

REILLY

                    Yes, when she's gone.

JULIA

Will Alex be here?

REILLY

          Yes, he'll be here.
                    [*Exit* JULIA *by side door*]
          [REILLY *presses button.*
NURSE-SECRETARY *shows in* CELIA.]

REILLY

Miss Celia Coplestone? . . . Won't you sit down?
I believe you are a friend of Mrs. Shuttlethwaite.

CELIA

Yes, it was Julia . . . Mrs. Shuttlethwaite
Who advised me to come to you. — But I've met you before,
Haven't I, somewhere? . . . Oh, of course.
But I didn't know . . .

REILLY

          There is nothing you need to know.
I was there at the instance of Mrs. Shuttlethwaite.

CELIA

That makes it even more perplexing. However,
I don't want to waste your time. And I'm awfully afraid
That you'll think that I am wasting it anyway.

I suppose most people, when they come to see you,
Are obviously ill, or can give good reasons
For wanting to see you. Well, I can't.
I just came in desperation. And I shan't be offended
If you simply tell me to go away again.

### REILLY

Most of my patients begin, Miss Coplestone,
By telling me exactly what is the matter with them,
And what I am to do about it. They are quite sure
They have had a nervous breakdown — that is what they
        call it —
And usually they think that someone else is to blame.

### CELIA

I at least have no one to blame but myself.

### REILLY

And after that, the prologue to my treatment
Is to try to show them that they are mistaken
About the nature of their illness, and lead them to see
That it's not so interesting as they had imagined.
When I get as far as that, there is something to be done.

### CELIA

Well, I can't pretend that my trouble is interesting;
But I shan't begin that way. I feel perfectly well.
I could lead an active life — if there's anything to work for;
I don't imagine that I am being persecuted;
I don't hear any voices, I have no delusions —
Except that the world I live in seems all a delusion!
But oughtn't I first to tell you the circumstances?
I'd forgotten that you know nothing about me;
And with what I've been going through, these last weeks,
I somehow took it for granted that I needn't explain myself.

REILLY

I know quite enough about you for the moment:
Try first to describe your present state of mind.

CELIA

Well, there are two things I can't understand,
Which you might consider symptoms. But first I must tell
    you
That I should really *like* to think there's something wrong
    with me —
Because, if there isn't, then there's something wrong,
Or at least, very different from what it seemed to be,
With the world itself — and that's much more frightening!
That would be terrible. So I'd rather believe
There is something wrong with me, that could be put right.
I'd do anything you told me, to get back to normality.

REILLY

We must find out about you, before we decide
What *is* normality.   You say there are two things:
What is the first?

CELIA
             An awareness of solitude.
But that sounds so flat. I don't mean simply
That there's been a crash: though indeed there has been.
It isn't simply the end of an illusion
In the ordinary way, or being ditched.
Of course that's something that's always happening
To all sorts of people, and they get over it
More or less, or at least they carry on.
No. I mean that what has happened has made me aware
That I've always been alone. That one always is alone.
Not simply the ending of one relationship,

Not even simply finding that it never existed —
But a revelation about my relationship
With *everybody*. Do you know —
It no longer seems worth while to *speak* to anyone!

REILLY

And what about your parents?

CELIA
                    Oh, they live in the country,
Now they can't afford to have a place in town.
It's all they can do to keep the country house going;
But it's been in the family so long, they won't leave it.

REILLY

And you live in London?

CELIA
I share a flat
With a cousin: but she's abroad at the moment,
And my family want me to come down and stay with them.
But I just can't face it.

REILLY
So you want to see no one?

CELIA
No . . . it isn't that I *want* to be alone,
But that everyone's alone — or so it seems to me.
They make noises, and think they are talking to each other;
They make faces, and think they understand each other.
And I'm sure that they don't. Is that a delusion?

131

REILLY

A delusion is something we must return from.
There are other states of mind,   which we take to be delusion,
But which we have to accept and go on from.
And the second symptom?

CELIA

                    That's stranger still.
It sounds ridiculous — but the only word for it
That I can find, is a sense of sin.

REILLY

You suffer from a sense of sin, Miss Coplestone?
This is most unusual.

CELIA

                    It seemed to *me* abnormal.

REILLY

We have yet to find what would be normal
For *you*, before we use the term 'abnormal'.
Tell me what you mean by a sense of sin.

CELIA

It's much easier to tell you what I don't mean:
I don't mean sin in the ordinary sense.

REILLY

And what, in your opinion, is the ordinary sense?

CELIA

Well . . . I suppose it's being immoral —
And I don't feel as if I was immoral:

132

In fact, aren't the people one thinks of as immoral
Just the people who we say have no moral sense?
I've never noticed that immorality
Was accompanied by a sense of sin:
At least, I have never come across it.
I suppose it is wicked to hurt other people.
If you know that you're hurting them. I haven't hurt *her*.
I wasn't taking anything away from her —
Anything she wanted. I may have been a fool:
But I don't mind at all having been a fool.

REILLY

And what is the point of view of your family?

CELIA

Well, my bringing up was pretty conventional —
I had always been taught to disbelieve in sin.
Oh, I don't mean that it was ever mentioned!
But anything wrong, from our point of view,
Was either bad form, or was psychological.
And bad form always led to disaster
Because the people one knew disapproved of it.
I don't worry much about form, myself —
But when everything's bad form, or mental kinks,
You either become bad form, and cease to care,
Or else, if you care, you must be kinky.

REILLY

And so you suppose you have what you call a 'kink'?

CELIA

But everything seemed so right, at the time!
I've been thinking about it, over and over;
I can see now, it was all a mistake.

But I don't see why mistakes should make one feel sinful!
And yet I can't find any other word for it.
It must be some kind of hallucination;
Yet, at the same time, I'm frightened by the fear
That it is more real than anything I believed in.

REILLY

What is more real than anything you believed in?

CELIA

It's not the feeling of anything I've ever *done*,
Which I might get away from, or of anything in me
I could get rid of — but of emptiness, of failure
Towards someone, or something, outside of myself;
And I feel I must . . . *atone* — is that the word?
Can you treat a patient for such a state of mind?

REILLY

What had you believed were your relations with this man?

CELIA

Oh, you'd guessed that, had you? That's clever of you.
No, perhaps I made it obvious. You don't need to know
About him, do you?

REILLY

No.

CELIA

Perhaps I'm only typical.

REILLY

There are different types. Some are rarer than others.

134

CELIA

Oh, I thought that I was giving him so much!
And he to me — and the giving and the taking
Seemed so right: not in terms of calculation
Of what was good for the persons we had been
But for the new person, *us*. If I could feel
As I did then, even now it would seem right.
And then I found we were only strangers
And that there had been neither giving nor taking
But that we had merely made use of each other
Each for his purpose. That's horrible. Can we only love
Something created by our own imagination?
Are we all in fact unloving and unlovable?
Then one *is* alone, and if one is alone
Then lover and belovèd are equally unreal
And the dreamer is no more real than his dreams.

REILLY

And this man. What does he now seem like, to you?

CELIA

Like a child who has wandered into a forest
Playing with an imaginary playmate
And suddenly discovers he is only a child
Lost in a forest, wanting to go home.

REILLY

Compassion may be already a clue
Towards finding your own way out of the forest.

CELIA

But even if I find my way out of the forest
I shall be left with the inconsolable memory
Of the treasure I went into the forest to find

135

And never found, and which was not there
And perhaps is not anywhere? But if not anywhere,
Why do I feel guilty at not having found it?

REILLY

Disillusion can become itself an illusion
If we rest in it.

CELIA
                I cannot argue.
It's not that I'm afraid of being hurt again:
Nothing again can either hurt or heal.
I have thought at moments that the ecstasy is real
Although those who experience it may have no reality.
For what happened is remembered like a dream
In which one is exalted by intensity of loving
In the spirit, a vibration of delight
Without desire, for desire is fulfilled
In the delight of loving. A state one does not know
When awake. But what, or whom I loved,
Or what in me was loving, I do not know.
And if that is all meaningless, I want to be cured
Of a craving for something I cannot find
And of the shame of never finding it.
Can you cure me?

REILLY
            The condition is curable.
But the form of treatment must be your own choice:
I cannot choose for you. If that is what you wish,
I can reconcile you to the human condition,
The condition to which some who have gone as far as you
Have succeeded in returning.  They may remember
The vision they have had, but they cease to regret it,

Maintain themselves by the common routine,
Learn to avoid excessive expectation,
Become tolerant of themselves and others,
Giving and taking, in the usual actions
What there is to give and take. They do not repine;
Are contented with the morning that separates
And with the evening that brings together
For casual talk before the fire
Two people who know they do not understand each other,
Breeding children whom they do not understand
And who will never understand them.

CELIA

        Is that the best life?

REILLY

It is a good life. Though you will not know how good
Till you come to the end. But you will want nothing else,
And the other life will be only like a book
You have read once, and lost. In a world of lunacy,
Violence, stupidity, greed . . . it is a good life.

CELIA

I know I ought to be able to accept that
If I might still have it. Yet it leaves me cold.
Perhaps that's just a part of my illness,
But I feel it would be a kind of surrender —
No, not a surrender — more like a betrayal.
You see, I think I really had a vision of something
Though I don't know what it is. I don't want to forget it.
I want to live with it. I could do without everything,
Put up with anything, if I might cherish it.
In fact, I think it would really be dishonest
For me, now, to try to make a life with *any*body!

137

I couldn't give anyone the kind of love —
I wish I could — which belongs to that life.
Oh, I'm afraid this sounds like raving!
Or just cantankerousness . . . still,
If there's no other way . . . then I feel just hopeless.

REILLY

There *is* another way, if you have the courage.
The first I could describe in familiar terms
Because you have seen it, as we all have seen it,
Illustrated, more or less, in lives of those about us.
The second is unknown, and so requires faith —
The kind of faith that issues from despair.
The destination cannot be described;
You will know very little until you get there;
You will journey blind. But the way leads towards possession
Of what you have sought for in the wrong place.

CELIA

That sounds like what I want. But what is my duty?

REILLY

Whichever way you choose will prescribe its own duty.

CELIA

Which way is better?

REILLY
                    Neither way is better.
Both ways are necessary. It is also necessary
To make a choice between them.

CELIA
                    Then I choose the second.

138

REILLY

It is a terrifying journey.

CELIA

                    I am not frightened
But glad. I suppose it is a lonely way?

REILLY

No lonelier than the other. But those who take the other
Can forget their loneliness. You will not forget yours.
Each way means loneliness — and communion.
Both ways avoid the final desolation
Of solitude in the phantasmal world
Of imagination, shuffling memories and desires.

CELIA

That is the hell I have been in.

REILLY

                    It isn't hell
Till you become incapable of anything else.
Now — do you feel quite sure?

CELIA

                    I want your second way.
So what am I to do?

REILLY

You will go to the sanatorium.

CELIA

Oh, what an anti-climax! I have known people
Who have been to your sanatorium, and come back again —
I don't mean to say they weren't much better for it —
That's why I came to you. But they returned . . .
Well . . . I mean . . . to everyday life.

139

REILLY

True. But the friends you have in mind
Cannot have been to this sanatorium.
I am very careful whom I send there:
Those who go do not come back as these did.

CELIA

It sounds like a prison. But they can't *all* stay there!
I mean, it would make the place so over-crowded.

REILLY

Not very many go. But I said they did not come back
In the sense in which your friends came back.
I did not say they stayed there.

CELIA
                    What becomes of them?

REILLY

They choose, Miss Coplestone. Nothing is forced on them.
Some of them return, in a physical sense;
No one disappears. They lead very active lives
Very often, in the world.

CELIA
                    How soon will you send me there?

REILLY

How soon will you be ready?

CELIA
                    Tonight, by nine o'clock.

REILLY

Go home then, and make your preparations.

Here is the address for **you** to give your friends;
                    [*Writes on a slip of paper*]
You had better let your family know at once.
I will send a car for you at nine o'clock.


CELIA

What do I need to take with me?


REILLY
                    Nothing.
Everything you need will be provided for you,
And you will have no expenses at the sanatorium.


CELIA

I don't in the least know what I am doing
Or why I am doing it. There is nothing else to do:
That is the only reason.


REILLY
                    It is the best reason.


CELIA

But I know it is I who have made the decision:
I must tell you that. Oh, I almost forgot —
May I ask what your fee is?


REILLY
                    I have told my secretary
That there is no fee.


CELIA
                    But . . .

141

REILLY
For a case like yours
There is no fee.
[*Presses button*]


CELIA
You have been very kind.


REILLY
Go in peace, my daughter.
Work out your salvation with diligence.
[NURSE-SECRETARY *appears at door. Exit* CELIA
REILLY *dials on house-telephone.*]


REILLY
[*Into telephone*]
It is finished.   You can come in now.
[*Enter* JULIA *by side door*]
She will go far, that one.


JULIA
Very far, I think.
You do not need to tell me. I knew from the beginning.


REILLY
It's the other ones I am worried about.


JULIA
Nonsense, Henry. *I* shall keep an eye on them.


REILLY
To send them back: what have they to go back to?
To the stale food mouldering in the larder,
The stale thoughts mouldering in their minds.

142

Each unable to disguise his own meanness
From himself, because it is known to the other.
It's not the knowledge of the mutual treachery
But the knowledge that the other understands the motive —
Mirror to mirror, reflecting vanity.
I have taken a great risk.

JULIA
                    We must always take risks.
That is our destiny. Since you question the decision
What possible alternative can you imagine?

REILLY
None.

JULIA
            Very well then. We must take the risk.
All we could do was to give them the chance.
And now, when they are stripped naked to their souls
And can choose, whether to put on proper costumes
Or huddle quickly into new disguises,
They have, for the first time, somewhere to start from.
Oh, of course, they might just murder each other!
But I don't think they will do that. We shall see.
It's the thought of Celia that weighs upon my mind.

REILLY
Of Celia?

JULIA
        Of Celia.

REILLY
            But when I said just now
That she would go far, you agreed with me.

143

JULIA

Oh yes, she will go far. And we know where she is going.
But what do we know of the terrors of the journey?
You and I don't know the process by which the human is
Transhumanised: what do we know
Of the kind of suffering they must undergo
On the way of illumination?

REILLY

Will she be frightened
By the first appearance of projected spirits?

JULIA

Henry, you simply do not understand innocence.
She will be afraid of nothing; she will not even know
That there is anything there to be afraid of.
She is too humble. She will pass between the scolding hills,
Through the valley of derision, like a child sent on an errand
In eagerness and patience. Yet she must suffer.

REILLY

When I express confidence in anything
You always raise doubts; when I am apprehensive
Then you see no reason for anything but confidence.

JULIA

That's one way in which I am so useful to you.
You ought to be grateful.

REILLY

And when I say to one like her
'Work out your salvation with diligence', I do not
understand
What I myself am saying.

JULIA
You must accept your limitations.
— But how much longer will Alex keep us waiting?

REILLY
He should be here by now. I'll speak to Miss Barraway.
[*Takes up house-telephone*]
Miss Barraway, when Mr. Gibbs arrives . . .
Oh, very good.
[*To* JULIA]
He's on his way up.
[*Into telephone*]
You may bring the tray in now, Miss Barraway.
[*Enter* ALEX]

ALEX
Well! Well! and how have we got on?

JULIA
Everything is in order.

ALEX
The Chamberlaynes have chosen?

REILLY
They accept their destiny.

ALEX
And *she* has made the choice?

REILLY
She will be fetched this evening.
[NURSE-SECRETARY *enters with a tray, a decanter and three
    glasses, and exit.* REILLY *pours drinks.*]
And now we are ready to proceed to the libation.

145

ALEX

The words for the building of the hearth.
                    [*They raise their glasses*]

REILLY

Let them build the hearth
Under the protection of the stars.

ALEX

Let them place a chair each side of it.

JULIA

May the holy ones watch over the roof,
May the Moon herself influence the bed.
                    [*They drink*]

ALEX

The words for those who go upon a journey.

REILLY

Protector of travellers
Bless the road.

ALEX

Watch over her in the desert.
Watch over her in the mountain.
Watch over her in the labyrinth.
Watch over her by the quicksand.

JULIA

Protect her from the Voices
Protect her from the Visions
Protect her in the tumult
Protect her in the silence.
                    [*They drink*]

146

REILLY

There is one for whom the words cannot be spoken.

ALEX

They can not be spoken yet.

JULIA

You mean Peter Quilpe.

REILLY

He has not yet come to where the words are valid.

JULIA

Shall we ever speak them?

ALEX

Others, perhaps, will speak them.
You know, I have connections — even in California.

CURTAIN

# Act Three

*The drawing-room of the Chamberlaynes' London flat. Two*
*years later. A late afternoon in July. A* CATERER'S
MAN *is arranging a buffet table.* LAVINIA *enters from*
*side door.*

CATERER'S MAN
Have you any further orders for us, Madam?

LAVINIA
You could bring in the trolley with the glasses
And leave them ready.

CATERER'S MAN
Very good, Madam.
[*Exit.* LAVINIA *looks about the room critically and moves*
*bowl of flowers.*]
[*Re-enter* CATERER'S MAN *with trolley*]

LAVINIA
There, in that corner. That's the most convenient;
You can get in and out. Is there anything you need
That you can't find in the kitchen?

CATERER'S MAN
Nothing, Madam.
Will there be anything more you require?

LAVINIA

Nothing more, I think, till half past six.

[*Exit* CATERER'S MAN]

[EDWARD *lets himself in at the front door*]

EDWARD

I'm in good time, I think. I hope you've not been worrying.

LAVINIA

Oh no. I did in fact ring up your chambers,
And your clerk told me you had already left.
But all I rang up for was to reassure you . . .

EDWARD

[*Smiling*]

That you hadn't run away?

LAVINIA

Now Edward, that's unfair!

You know that we've given *several* parties
In the last two years. And I've attended *all* of them.
I hope you're not too tired?

EDWARD

Oh no, a quiet day.

Two consultations with solicitors
On quite straightforward cases. It's you who should be tired.

LAVINIA

I'm not tired yet. But I know that I'll be glad
When it's all over.

EDWARD

I like the dress you're wearing:

I'm glad you put on that one.

LAVINIA

Well, Edward!
Do you know it's the first time you've paid me a compliment
*Before* a party? And that's when one needs them.

EDWARD

Well, you deserve it. — We asked too many people.

LAVINIA

It's true, a great many more accepted
Than we thought would want to come. But what can you do?
There's usually a lot who don't want to come
But all the same would be bitterly offended
To hear we'd given a party without asking them.

EDWARD

Perhaps we ought to have arranged to have two parties
Instead of one.

LAVINIA

That's never satisfactory.
Everyone who's asked to either party
Suspects that the other one was more important.

EDWARD

That's true. You have a very practical mind.

LAVINIA

But you know, I don't think that you need worry:
They won't all come, out of those who accepted.
You know we said, 'we can ask twenty more
Because they will be going to the Gunnings instead'.

EDWARD

I know, that's what we said at the time;
But I'd forgotten what the Gunnings' parties were like.
Their guests will get just enough to make them thirsty;
They'll come on to us later, roaring for drink.
Well, let's hope that those who come to us early
Will be going on to the Gunnings afterwards,
To make room for those who come from the Gunnings.

LAVINIA

And if it's very crowded, they can't get at the cocktails,
And the man won't be able to take the tray about,
So they'll go away again. Anyway, at that stage
There's nothing whatever you can do about it:
And everyone likes to be seen at a party
Where everybody else is, to show they've been invited.
That's what makes it a success. Is that picture straight?

EDWARD

Yes, it is.

LAVINIA

No, it isn't. Do please straighten it.

EDWARD

Is it straight now?

LAVINIA

Too much to the left.

EDWARD

How's that now?

LAVINIA

No, I meant the right.
That will do. I'm too tired to bother.

EDWARD

After they're all gone, we will have some champagne.
Just ourselves. You lie down now, Lavinia.
No one will be coming for at least half an hour;
So just stretch out.

LAVINIA

You must sit beside me,
Then I can relax.

EDWARD

This is the best moment
Of the whole party.

LAVINIA

Oh no, Edward.
The best moment is the moment it's over;
And then to remember, it's the end of the season
And no more parties.

EDWARD

And no more committees.

LAVINIA

Can we get away soon?

EDWARD

By the end of next week
I shall be quite free.

LAVINIA
And we can be alone.
I love that house being so remote.

EDWARD
That's why we took it. And I'm really thankful
To have that excuse for not seeing people;
And you do need to rest now.
　　　　　[*The doorbell rings*]

LAVINIA
Oh, bother!
Now who would come so early? I simply *can't* get up.

CATERER'S MAN
Mrs. Shuttlethwaite!

LAVINIA
Oh, it's Julia!
[*Enter* JULIA]

JULIA
Well, my dears, and here I am!
I seem *literally* to have caught you napping!
I know I'm much too early; but the fact is, my dears,
That I have to go on to the Gunnings' party —
And you know what *they* offer in the way of food and drink!
And I've had to miss my tea, and I'm simply ravenous
And dying of thirst. What can Parkinson's do for me?
Oh yes, I know this is a Parkinson party;
I recognised one of their men at the door —
An old friend of mine, in fact. But I'm forgetting!
I've got a surprise: I've brought Alex with me!
He only got back this morning from somewhere —

153

One of his mysterious expeditions,
And we're going to get him to tell us all about it.
But what's become of him?
[*Enter* ALEX]

                    EDWARD
                Well, Alex!
Where on earth do you turn up from?

                    ALEX
Where on earth? From the east. From Kinkanja —
An island that you won't have heard of
Yet. Got back this morning. I heard about your party
And, as I thought you might be leaving for the country,
I said, I must not miss the opportunity
To see Edward and Lavinia.

                    LAVINIA
                How are you, Alex?

                    ALEX
I did try to get you on the telephone
After lunch, but my secretary couldn't get through to you.
Never mind, I said — to myself, not to her —
Never mind: the unexpected guest
Is the one to whom they give the warmest welcome.
I know them well enough for that.

                    JULIA
                        But tell us, Alex.
What were you doing in this strange place —
What's it called?

                    ALEX
                Kinkanja.

JULIA

What were you doing
In Kinkanja? Visiting some Sultan?
You were shooting tigers?

ALEX

There are no tigers, Julia,
In Kinkanja. And there are no sultans.
I have been staying with the Governor.
Three of us have been out on a tour of inspection
Of local conditions.

JULIA

What about? Monkey nuts?

ALEX

That was a nearer guess than you think.
No, not monkey nuts. But it had to do with monkeys —
Though whether the monkeys are the core of the problem
Or merely a symptom, I am not so sure.
At least, the monkeys have become the pretext
For general unrest amongst the natives.

EDWARD

But how do the monkeys create unrest?

ALEX

To begin with, the monkeys are very destructive . . .

JULIA

You don't need to tell me that monkeys are destructive.
I shall never forget Mary Mallington's monkey,
The horrid little beast — stole my ticket to Mentone
And I had to travel in a very slow train

And in a *couchette*. She was very angry
When I told her the creature ought to be destroyed.

LAVINIA

But can't they exterminate these monkeys
If they are a pest?

ALEX

Unfortunately,
The majority of the natives are heathen:
They hold these monkeys in peculiar veneration
And do not want them killed. So they blame the
          Government
For the damage that the monkeys do.

EDWARD

That seems unreasonable.

ALEX

It is unreasonable,
But characteristic. And that's not the worst of it.
Some of the tribes are Christian converts,
And, naturally, take a different view.
They trap the monkeys. And they eat them.
The young monkeys are extremely palatable:
I've cooked them myself . . .

EDWARD

And did anybody eat them
When you cooked them?

ALEX

Oh yes, indeed.
I invented for the natives several new recipes.

156

But you see, what with eating the monkeys
And what with protecting their crops from the monkeys
The Christian natives prosper exceedingly:
And that creates friction between them and the others.
And that's the real problem. I hope I'm not boring you?

EDWARD

No indeed: we are anxious to learn the solution.

ALEX

I'm not sure that there *is* any solution.
But even this does not bring us to the heart of the matter.
There are also foreign agitators,
Stirring up trouble . . .

LAVINIA
Why don't you expel them?

ALEX

They are citizens of a friendly neighbouring state
Which we have just recognised. You see, Lavinia,
There are very deep waters.

EDWARD
And the agitators;
How do they agitate?

ALEX
By convincing the heathen
That the slaughter of monkeys has put a curse on them
Which can only be removed by slaughtering the Christians.
They have even been persuading some of the converts —
Who, after all, prefer not to be slaughtered —

To relapse into heathendom. So, instead of eating monkeys
They are eating Christians.

 JULIA

Who have eaten monkeys.

ALEX

The native is not, I fear, very logical.

JULIA

I wondered where you were taking us, with your monkeys.
I thought I was going to dine out on those monkeys:
But one can't dine out on eating Christians —
Even among pagans!

ALEX

Not on the *whole* story.

EDWARD

And have any of the English residents been murdered?

ALEX

Yes, but they are not usually eaten.
When these people have done with a European
He is, as a rule, no longer fit to eat.

EDWARD

And what has your commission accomplished?

ALEX

We have just drawn up an interim report.

EDWARD

Will it be made public?

ALEX

It cannot be, at present:
There are too many international complications.
Eventually, there may be an official publication.

EDWARD

But when?

ALEX

In a year or two.

EDWARD

And meanwhile?

ALEX

Meanwhile the monkeys multiply.

LAVINIA

And the Christians?

ALEX

Ah, the Christians! Now, I think I ought to tell you
About someone you know — or knew . . .

JULIA

Edward!

Somebody must have walked over my grave:
I'm feeling so chilly. Give me some gin.
Not a cocktail. I'm freezing — in July!

CATERER'S MAN

Mr. Quilpe!

EDWARD

Now who . . .

[*Enter* PETER]

Why, it's Peter!

LAVINIA

Peter!

PETER

Hullo, everybody!

LAVINIA

When did you arrive?

PETER

I flew over from New York last night —
I left Los Angeles three days ago.
I saw Sheila Paisley at lunch to-day
And she told me you were giving a party —
She's coming on later, after the Gunnings —
So I said, I really must crash in:
It's my only chance to see Edward and Lavinia.
I'm only over for a week, you see,
And I'm driving down to the country this evening,
So I knew you wouldn't mind my looking in so early.
It does seem ages since I last saw any of you!
And how are you, Alex? And dear old Julia!

LAVINIA

So you've just come from New York.

PETER

Yes, from New York.
The Bologolomskys saw me off.

160

You remember Princess Bologolomsky
In the old days? We dined the other night
At the Saffron Monkey. That's the place to go now.

ALEX

How very odd. *My* monkeys are saffron.

PETER

Your monkeys, Alex? I always said
That Alex knew everybody. But I didn't know
That he knew any monkeys.

JULIA

　　　　　　But give us your news;
Give us your news of the world, Peter.
We lead such a quiet life, here in London.

PETER

You always did enjoy a leg-pull, Julia:
But you all know I'm working for Pan-Am-Eagle?

EDWARD

No. Tell us, what is Pan-Am-Eagle?

PETER

You must have been living a quiet life!
Don't you go to the movies?

LAVINIA

　　　　Occasionally.

PETER

　　　　　　　　　Alex knows.
Did you see my last picture, Alex?

ALEX

I knew about it, but I didn't see it.
There is no cinema in Kinkanja.

PETER

Kinkanja? Where's that? They don't have pictures?
Pan-Am-Eagle must look into this.
Perhaps it would be a good place to make one.
— Alex knows all about Pan-Am-Eagle:
It was he who introduced me to the great Bela.

JULIA

And who is the great Bela?

PETER

Why, Bela Szogody —
He's my boss. I thought everyone knew *his* name.

JULIA

Is he your connection in California, Alex?

ALEX

Yes, we have sometimes obliged each other.

PETER

Well, it was Bela sent me over
Just for a week. And I have my hands full
I'm going down tonight, to Boltwell.

JULIA

To stay with the Duke?

PETER

And do him a good turn.
We're making a film of English life
And we want to use Boltwell.

162

JULIA

But I understood that Boltwell
Is in a very decayed condition.

PETER

Exactly. It is. And that's why we're interested.
The most decayed noble mansion in England!
At least, of any that are still inhabited.
We've got a team of experts over
To study the decay, so as to reproduce it.
Then we build another Boltwell in California.

JULIA

But what is your position, Peter?
Have you become an expert on decaying houses?

PETER

Oh dear no! I've written the script of this film,
And Bela is very pleased with it.
He thought I should see the original Boltwell;
And besides, he thought that as I'm English
I ought to know the best way to handle a duke.
Besides that, we've got the casting director:
He's looking for some typical English faces —
Of course, only for minor parts —
And I'll help him decide what faces are typical.

JULIA

Peter, I've thought of a wonderful idea!
I've always wanted to go to California:
Couldn't you persuade your casting director
To take us all over? We're all very typical.

PETER

No, I'm afraid . . .

163

CATERER'S MAN
Sir Henry Harcourt-Reilly!


JULIA
Oh, I forgot! I'd another surprise for you.
[*Enter* REILLY]
I want you to meet Sir Henry Harcourt-Reilly —


EDWARD
We're delighted to see him. But we *have* met before.


JULIA
Then if you know him already, you won't be afraid of him.
You know, I was afraid of him at first:
He looks so forbidding . . .


REILLY
My dear Julia,
You are giving me a very bad introduction —
Supposing that an introduction was necessary.


JULIA
My dear Henry, you are interrupting me.


LAVINIA
If you can interrupt Julia, Sir Henry,
You are the perfect guest we've been looking for.


REILLY
I should not dream of trying to interrupt Julia . . .


JULIA
But you're both interrupting!

REILLY
Who is interrupting now?

JULIA
Well, you shouldn't interrupt my interruptions:
That's really worse than interrupting.
Now my head's fairly spinning. I must have a cocktail.

EDWARD
[*To* REILLY]
And will you have a cocktail?

REILLY
Might I have a glass of water?

EDWARD
Anything with it?

REILLY
Nothing, thank you.

LAVINIA
May I introduce Mr. Peter Quilpe?
Sir Henry Harcourt-Reilly. Peter's an old friend
Of my husband and myself. Oh, I forgot —
[*Turning to* ALEX]
I rather assumed that you knew each other —
I don't know why I should. Mr. MacColgie Gibbs.

ALEX
Indeed, yes, we have met.

REILLY
On several commissions.

JULIA

We've been having such an interesting conversation.
Peter's just over from California
Where he's something very important in films.
He's making a film of English life
And he's going to find parts for all of us. Think of it!

PETER

But, Julia, I was just about to explain —
I'm afraid I can't find parts for anybody
In *this* film — it's not my business;
And that's not the way we do it.

JULIA

                    But, Peter;
If you're taking Boltwell to California
Why can't you take me?

PETER

                    We're not taking Boltwell.
We reconstruct a Boltwell.

JULIA

                    Very well, then:
Why not reconstruct *me*? It's very much cheaper.
Oh, dear, I can see you're determined not to have me:
So good-bye to my hopes of seeing California.

PETER

You know you'd never come if we invited you.
But there's someone I wanted to ask about,
Who did really want to get into films,
And I always thought she could make a success of it
If she only got the chance. It's Celia Coplestone.

166

She always wanted to. And now I could help her.
I've already spoken to Bela about her,
And I want to introduce her to our casting director.
I've got an idea for another film.
Can you tell me where she is? I couldn't find her
In the telephone directory.

JULIA

Not in the directory,
Or in any directory. You can tell them now, Alex.

LAVINIA

What does Julia mean?

ALEX

I was about to speak of her
When you came in, Peter. I'm afraid you can't have Celia.

PETER

Oh . . . Is she married?

ALEX

Not married, but dead.

LAVINIA

Celia?

ALEX

Dead.

PETER

Dead. That knocks the bottom out of it.

EDWARD

Celia dead.

167

JULIA

You had better tell them, Alex,
The news that you bring back from Kinkanja.

LAVINIA

Kinkanja? What was Celia doing in Kinkanja?
We heard that she had joined some nursing order . . .

ALEX

She had joined an order. A very austere one.
And as she already had experience of nursing . . .

LAVINIA

Yes, she had been a V.A.D. I remember.

ALEX

She was directed to Kinkanja,
Where there are various endemic diseases
Besides, of course, those brought by Europeans,
And where the conditions are favourable to plague.

EDWARD

Go on.

ALEX

It seems that there were three of them —
Three sisters at this station, in a Christian village;
And half the natives were dying of pestilence.
They must have been overworked for weeks.

EDWARD

And then?

ALEX

And then, the insurrection broke out
Among the heathen, of which I was telling you.

They knew of it, but would not leave the dying natives.
Eventually, two of them escaped:
One died in the jungle, and the other
Will never be fit for normal life again.
But Celia Coplestone, she was taken.
When our people got there, they questioned the villagers —
Those who survived. And then they found her body,
Or at least, they found the traces of it.

EDWARD

But before that . . .

ALEX
It was difficult to tell.
But from what we know of local practices
It would seem that she must have been crucified
Very near an ant-hill.

LAVINIA
But Celia! . . . Of all people . . .

EDWARD

And just for a handful of plague-stricken natives
Who would have died anyway.

ALEX
Yes, the patients died anyway;
Being tainted with the plague, they were not eaten.

LAVINIA

Oh, Edward, I'm so sorry — what a feeble thing to say!
But you know what I mean.

EDWARD
And you know what I'm thinking.

169

PETER

I don't understand at all.   But then I've been away
For two years, and don't know what happened
To Celia, during those two years.
Two years! Thinking about Celia.

EDWARD

It's the waste that I resent.

PETER

                          You know more than I do:
For *me*, it's everything else that's a waste.
Two years! And it was all a mistake.
Julia! Why don't *you* say anything?

JULIA

You gave her those two years, as best you could.

PETER

When did she . . . take up this career?

JULIA

                                   Two years ago.

PETER

Two years ago! I tried to forget about her,
Until I began to think myself a success
And got a little more self-confidence;
And then I thought about her again. More and more.
At first I did not want to know about Celia
And so I never asked. Then I wanted to know
And did not dare to ask. It took all my courage
To ask you about her just now; but I never thought
Of anything like this. I suppose I didn't know her,
I didn't understand her. I understand nothing.

170

REILLY

You understand your *métier*, Mr. Quilpe —
Which is the most that any of us can ask for.

PETER

And what a *métier*! I've tried to believe in it
So that I might believe in myself.
I thought I had ideas to make a revolution
In the cinema, that no one could ignore —
And here I am, making a second-rate film!
But I thought it was going to lead to something better,
And that seemed possible, while Celia was alive.
I wanted it, believed in it, for Celia.
And, of course, I wanted to do something for Celia —
But what mattered was, that Celia was alive.
And now it's all worthless. Celia's not alive.

LAVINIA

No, it's not all worthless, Peter. You've only just begun.
I mean, this only brings you to the point
At which you *must* begin. You were saying just now
That you never knew Celia. We none of us did.
What you've been living on is an image of Celia
Which you made for yourself, to meet your own needs.
Peter, please don't think I'm being unkind . . .

PETER

No, I don't think you're being unkind, Lavinia;
And I know that you're right.

LAVINIA

                              And perhaps what I've been saying
Will seem less unkind if I can make you understand
That in fact I've been talking about myself.

171

EDWARD

Lavinia is right. This is where you start from.
If you find out now, Peter, things about yourself
That you don't like to face: well, just remember
That some men have to learn much worse things
About themselves, and learn them later
When it's harder to recover, and make a new beginning.
It's not so hard for you. You're naturally good.

PETER

I'm sorry. I don't believe I've taken in
All that you've been saying. But I'm grateful all the same.
You know, all the time that you've been talking,
One thought has been going round and round in my head —
That I've only been interested in myself:
And that isn't good enough for Celia.

JULIA

You must have learned how to look at people, Peter,
When you look at them with an eye for the films:
That is, when you're not concerned with yourself
But just being an eye. You will come to think of Celia
Like that, one day. And then you'll understand her
And be reconciled, and be happy in the thought of her.

LAVINIA

Sir Henry, there is something I want to say to you.
While Alex was telling us what had happened to Celia
I was looking at your face. And it seemed from your
        expression
That the way in which she died did not disturb you
Or the fact that she died because she would not leave
A few dying natives.

REILLY

Who knows, Mrs. Chamberlayne,
The difference that made to the natives who were dying
Or the state of mind in which they died?

LAVINIA

I'm willing to grant that. What struck me, though,
Was that your face showed no surprise or horror
At the way in which she died. I don't know if you knew her.
I suspect that you did. In any case you knew *about* her.
Yet I thought your expression was one of . . . satisfaction!

REILLY

Mrs. Chamberlayne, I must be very transparent
Or else you are very perceptive.

JULIA

Oh, Henry!
Lavinia is much more observant than you think.
I believe that she has forced you to a show-down.

REILLY

You state the position correctly, Julia.
Do you mind if I quote poetry, Mrs. Chamberlayne?

LAVINIA

Oh no, I should love to hear you speaking poetry . . .

JULIA

She has made a point, Henry.

LAVINIA

. . . if it answers my question.

REILLY

   *Ere Babylon was dust*
*The magus Zoroaster, my dead child,*
*Met his own image walking in the garden.*
*That apparition, sole of men, he saw.*
*For know there are two worlds of life and death:*
*One that which thou beholdest; but the other*
*Is underneath the grave, where do inhabit*
*The shadows of all forms that think and live*
*Till death unite them and they part no more!*

When I first met Miss Coplestone, in this room,
I saw the image, standing behind her chair,
Of a Celia Coplestone whose face showed the astonishment
Of the first five minutes after a violent death.
If this strains your credulity, Mrs. Chamberlayne,
I ask you only to entertain the suggestion
That a sudden intuition, in certain minds,
May tend to express itself at once in a picture.
That happens to me, sometimes. So it was obvious
That here was a woman under sentence of death.
That was her destiny. The only question
Then was, what sort of death?  *I* could not know;
Because it was for her to choose the way of life
To lead to death, and, without knowing the end
Yet choose the form of death. We know the death she chose.
I did not know that she would die in this way;
*She* did not know. So all that I could do
Was to direct her in the way of preparation.
That way, which she accepted, led to this death.
And if that is not a happy death, what death is happy?

EDWARD

Do you mean that having chosen this form of death

She did not suffer as ordinary people suffer?

REILLY

Not at all what I mean. Rather the contrary.
I'd say that she suffered all that we should suffer
In fear and pain and loathing — all these together —
And reluctance of the body to become a *thing*.
I'd say she suffered more, because more conscious
Than the rest of us. She paid the highest price
In suffering. That is part of the design.

LAVINIA

Perhaps she had been through greater agony beforehand.
I mean — I know nothing of her last two years.

REILLY

That shows some insight on your part, Mrs. Chamberlayne;
But such experience can only be hinted at
In myths and images. To speak about it
We talk of darkness, labyrinths, Minotaur terrors.
But that world does not take the place of this one.
Do you imagine that the Saint in the desert
With spiritual evil always at his shoulder
Suffered any less from hunger, damp, exposure,
Bowel trouble, and the fear of lions,
Cold of the night and heat of the day, than we should?

EDWARD

But if this was right — if this was right for Celia —
There must be something else that is terribly wrong,
And the rest of us are somehow involved in the wrong.
I should only speak for myself. I'm sure that *I* am.

REILLY

Let me free your mind from one impediment:

175

You must try to detach yourself from what you still feel
As your responsibility.

                    EDWARD
                        I cannot help the feeling
That, in some way, my responsibility
Is greater than that of a band of half-crazed savages.

                    LAVINIA
Oh, Edward, I knew! I knew what you were thinking!
Doesn't it help you, that I feel guilty too?

                    REILLY
If we were all judged according to the consequences
Of all our words and deeds, beyond the intention
And beyond our limited understanding
Of ourselves and others, we should all be condemned.
Mrs. Chamberlayne, I often have to make a decision
Which may mean restoration or ruin to a patient —
And sometimes I have made the wrong decision.
As for Miss Coplestone, because you think her death was waste
You blame yourselves, and because you blame yourselves
You think her life was wasted. It was triumphant.
But I am no more responsible for the triumph —
And just as responsible for her death as you are.

                    LAVINIA
Yet I know I shall go on blaming myself
For being so unkind to her . . . so spiteful.
I shall go on seeing her at the moment
When she said good-bye to us, two years ago.

                    EDWARD
Your responsibility is nothing to mine, Lavinia.

                        176

LAVINIA

I'm not sure about that. If I had understood you
Then I might not have misunderstood Celia.

REILLY

You will have to live with these memories and make them
Into something new. Only by acceptance
Of the past will you alter its meaning.

JULIA

Henry, I think it is time that *I* said something:
Everyone makes a choice, of one kind or another,
And then must take the consequences. Celia chose
A way of which the consequence was Kinkanja.
Peter chose a way that leads him to Boltwell:
And he's got to go there . . .

PETER

           I see what you mean.
I wish I didn't have to. But the car will be waiting,
And the experts — I'd almost forgotten them.
I realise that I can't get out of it —
And what else can I do?

ALEX

           It is your film.
And I know that Bela expects great things of it.

PETER

So now I'll be going.

EDWARD

           Shall we see you again, Peter,
Before you leave England?

LAVINIA

          Do try to come to see us.
You know, I think it would do us all good —
You and me and Edward . . . to talk about Celia

PETER

Thanks very much. But not this time —
I simply shan't be able to.

EDWARD

          But on your next visit?

PETER

The next time I come to England, I promise you.
I really do want to see you both, very much.
Good-bye, Julia. Good-bye, Alex. Good-bye, Sir Henry.

          [*Exit*]

JULIA

. . . And now the consequences of the Chamberlaynes' choice
Is a cocktail party. They must be ready for it.
Their guests may be arriving at any moment.

REILLY

Julia, you are right. It is also right
That the Chamberlaynes should now be giving a party.

LAVINIA

And I have been thinking, for these last five minutes,
How I could face my guests. I wish it was over.
I mean . . . I am glad you came . . . I am glad Alex told us . . .
And Peter had to know . . .

EDWARD

          Now I think I understand . . .

LAVINIA

Then I hope you will explain it to me!

EDWARD

                       Oh, it isn't much
That I understand yet! But Sir Henry has been saying,
I think, that every moment is a fresh beginning;
And Julia, that life is only keeping on;
And somehow, the two ideas seem to fit together.

LAVINIA

But all the same . . . I don't want to see these people.

REILLY

It is your appointed burden. And as for the party,
I am sure it will be a success.

JULIA

             And I think, Henry,
That we should leave before the party begins.
They will get on better without us. You too, Alex.

LAVINIA

We don't *want* you to go!

ALEX

             We have another engagement.

REILLY

And on this occasion I shall not be unexpected.

JULIA

Now, Henry. Now, Alex. We're going to the Gunnings.
                 [*Exeunt* JULIA, REILLY *and* ALEX]

179

LAVINIA

Edward, how am I looking?

EDWARD
Very well.
I might almost say, your best. But you always look your best.

LAVINIA

Oh, Edward, that spoils it. No woman can believe
That she always looks her best. You're rather transparent,
You know, when you're trying to cheer me up.
To say I always look my best can only mean the worst.

EDWARD

I never shall learn how to pay a compliment.

LAVINIA

What you should have done was to admire my dress.

EDWARD

But I've already told you how much I like it.

LAVINIA

But so much has happened since then. And besides,
One sometimes likes to hear the same compliment twice.

EDWARD

And now for the party.

LAVINIA
Now for the party.

EDWARD

It will soon be over.

LAVINIA
I wish it would begin.

EDWARD
There's the doorbell.

LAVINIA
Oh, I'm glad. It's begun.

CURTAIN

# Appendix

The tune of *One-Eyed Riley* (page 38), as scored from the author's dictation by Miss Mary Trevelyan.

As I was walk-ing round and round and round in ev'-ry quar-ter I walk'd in to a pub-lic house and or-der'd up my gin and wa-ter

REFRAIN

Too - ri - oo - ley, Too - ri - i - ley, What's the mat-ter with One-Eyed Ri - ley

As I was drink-in' gin and wa-ter (And me be-in' the One-Eyed Ri-ley) Who came in but the land-lord's daugh-ter And she took my heart en-tire-ly

REFRAIN

Too - ri - oo - ley, Too - ri - i - ley, What's the mat-ter with One-Eyed Ri - ley

# The Cast of the First Production
## at the
## Edinburgh Festival,
### August 22-27, 1949

| | |
|---|---|
| Edward Chamberlayne | ROBERT FLEMYNG |
| Julia (Mrs. Shuttlethwaite) | CATHLEEN NESBITT |
| Celia Coplestone | IRENE WORTH |
| Alexander McColgie Gibbs | ERNEST CLARK |
| Peter Quilpe | DONALD HOUSTON |
| An Unidentified Guest, *later identified* | |
| *as* Sir Henry Harcourt-Reilly | ALEC GUINNESS |
| Lavinia Chamberlayne | URSULA JEANS |
| A Nurse-Secretary | CHRISTINA HORNIMAN |
| Two Caterer's Men | { DONALD BAIN<br>MARTIN BECKWITH |

Directed by E. MARTIN BROWNE

Settings designed by ANTHONY HOLLAND

Produced by SHEREK PLAYERS LTD.

in association with THE ARTS COUNCIL